MW00379408

THE
KETO
MEAL PLAN
COOKBOOK

THE
KETO
MEAL PLAN
COOKBOOK

Lose Weight and Feel Great While
Saving Time and Money

**Lara Clevenger, MSH, RDN, CPT
& Faith Gorsky**

Skyhorse Publishing

Skyhorse Publishing books may be purchased in bulk at special discounts for sales promotion, corporate gifts, fund-raising, or educational purposes. Special editions can also be created to specifications. For details, contact the Special Sales Department, Skyhorse Publishing, 307 West 36th Street, 11th Floor, New York, NY 10018 or info@skyhorsepublishing.com.

Skyhorse® and Skyhorse Publishing® are registered trademarks of Skyhorse Publishing, Inc.®, a Delaware corporation.

Visit our website at www.skyhorsepublishing.com.

10 9 8 7 6 5 4 3

Library of Congress Cataloging-in-Publication Data is available on file.
Library of Congress Control Number: 2019953993

Cover design by Daniel Brount
Cover photo credit by Faith Gorsky
Interior photographs by Faith Gorsky

Print ISBN: 978-1-5107-4905-4
Ebook ISBN: 978-1-5107-4906-1

Printed in China

Contents

INTRODUCTION

Why You Should Meal Prep

One of the biggest factors that helps many of us succeed with our diet of choice, whether it is a ketogenic lifestyle or something else, is planning ahead. Because even though we start out with the best intentions, life happens! Like those evenings when you unexpectedly have to work late and there's only thirty minutes to get one kid to soccer practice and the other kid to a music lesson; at this point, the drive-through window of the nearest fast-food place can start to look pretty good! But if you're a meal planner and either have leftovers in the fridge or something you can quickly pull out of the freezer, you can easily get a nutritious meal on the dinner table for you and your family.

And let's get right to the point: some of the biggest reasons to plan and prep your meals are to save money and time, which meal prep allows! This book not only teaches you how to meal prep, but also takes the guesswork out of putting together a menu—we've already done that for you. All you have to do is follow it and start looking forward to home-cooked meals.

Another perk that comes along with meal prep is reduced food waste because you're only buying what you need and you're making better use of leftovers.

Last but not least, meal prep can be a great way to reach your health goals. When you plan ahead, you'll know you're putting healthy foods into your body! Planning, prepping, and eating nutrient-dense meals can more effectively help you to reach your weight loss and healthy living goals.

Meal planning and meal prep might initially seem like an overwhelming task and a chore, but in the end, it will make your daily life run smoother and actually open up more free time in the long run. But before we dive into meal prep, first let's talk a little bit about a ketogenic lifestyle and way of eating.

Keto Basics

What is keto? *Keto* is short for *ketogenic*, which in a nutshell refers to a state in which your body primarily uses ketones and fat for fuel instead of glucose and carbohydrates. *How do we get into a ketogenic state?* We do this by limiting our carbohydrate intake. You might be wondering, *How many carbs can I have and still be keto?* That depends on many different factors, including height, age, weight, activity level, metabolism, and chronic conditions. Typically, people can consume 5 to 10 percent of their calories from non-starchy carbohydrates and still stay in ketosis. Of course, this may change if you decide to binge and eat 10,000 calories—since that's a huge quantity of food, 5 to 10 percent of those calories from carbs may kick you out of ketosis.

A common question is: *How much fat do I need to eat to be keto?* This is based on the individual, too! Some people do fine with as little as 65 percent of calories from fat, while others need to consume upwards of 80 to 85 percent of calories from fat to feel their best. And if you're using a keto diet to treat a disease like epilepsy, you may even be instructed to consume up to 90 percent of your calories from fat. Typically, the higher percentage of calories consumed from fat, the higher blood ketone levels are, and the higher your energy level and the better you feel. However, there does seem to be an upper limit when it comes to maintainability. The higher the fat percentage in a diet, the harder it might be to maintain because that means you'll need to supplement your diet with lots of added fats, which can become tedious or boring.

Another important question is: *What about protein?* Once you find your sweet spot with the right amount of carbs and fat to maintain ketosis, protein fills in the rest. Protein or amino acids are the building blocks of our cells. They are integral to preserving lean body mass, which correlates to our metabolism. Typically, the leaner body mass (or muscle mass) a person has, the faster their metabolism is, which affects how many calories a person can burn at rest. However, this may not be the case if you have a history of extreme dieting and you have lowered your resting metabolic rate, which is known as RMR (also known as metabolism).

At this point, you might ask, *Why would a person want to follow a keto diet?* Many people turn to keto for weight loss when they hear their friends shouting from the rooftops about how it's helped them lose weight. Well, weight loss is just one of the many benefits that you can reap from a ketogenic diet! Other benefits may include better blood work, sleep, skin, and digestion, as well as health improvements for those who suffer from anxiety and insulin resistance. Research is still ongoing to locate other health benefits that a ketogenic lifestyle may provide.

Sources of Carbohydrates on a Keto Diet
Because the goal of a keto diet is to limit carbohydrates and to use fat as a main source of fuel for the body, which carbs can you eat? Quite a few, actually! You can eat mostly non-starchy vegetables like asparagus, green leafy vegetables, broccoli, cauliflower, Brussels sprouts, artichoke hearts, cabbage, etc. You can even fit in starchier vegetables like carrots—if you do so mindfully and in smaller amounts. Lower carb fruits like berries are also great! Additionally, fruit like coconut, olives, and avocado all work well on a keto diet—not only are they low in carbohydrates and packed full of vitamins and minerals, but they are also good sources of fat.

There are other foods that you might not necessarily think of as containing carbohydrates, such as dairy. High-fat dairy products, like cream and yogurt, can still be consumed on a keto diet; just look for higher-fat options and unsweetened versions. Also, some types of seafood, such as shellfish, contain carbohydrates. These can be consumed on a keto diet—mindfully. Nuts, seeds, and some legumes may also be consumed on a keto diet. Many of these contain carbohydrates, some in higher amounts than others. We tend to steer clear of processed keto foods and opt for whole foods. If you're into convenience foods, note that many of them may contain carbohydrates in the form of sweeteners, fibers, sugar alcohols, and binders, so just be sure to track these ingredients when developing your keto meal plan.

Sources of Protein on a Keto Diet
Protein sources on this diet include livestock, such as beef, lamb, goat, and pig;

poultry, such as chicken and turkey; other fowl, such as duck; wild game, such as venison; wild-caught fish (preference given to fattier varieties); and shellfish. Other less protein-rich sources include nuts, seeds, cheese, etc. Even vegetables contain a little bit of protein, but you'd probably go over your carbohydrate limit if you tried to get in enough protein from whole-food plant sources (unless you're consuming powders).

Fat Sources in a Keto Diet
Fatty cuts of meat and fattier varieties of fish should be the preferred fuel source. You can also cook your meat in fat, such as ghee, lard, tallow, duck fat, coconut oil, and avocado oil. Additionally, vegetarian fat sources include nuts and seeds, avocados, olives, and coconut.

KETO MEAL PREP MADE EASY

In this book we'll show you how to meal prep for success! If you can't already tell, we're huge fans of meal prepping, and there's a bunch of different ways you can make meal prep work for you. For example, you can cook individual proteins and veggies in bulk, and then mix and match them with sauces. Some people like to increase the serving size of their favorite recipes and eat it throughout the week as leftovers. Or you can just make a bunch of different dinners on the weekend and eat them as lunches and dinners during the week, or stash a few in your freezer for super-busy nights.

Meal Prep Techniques: Hands-Off Cooking Methods

Convenient cooking methods, such as using appliances like electric pressure cookers and slow cookers, will do the work for you, not even requiring you to stir! They are truly hands-off. Once you start to utilize these cooking methods, you'll realize that getting a nutritious meal on the table for your family doesn't have to be a chore.

Electric Pressure Cooker

Besides being a hands-off cooking method, the electric pressure cooker (such as an Instant Pot) cooks food in a fraction of the time that it would otherwise take. It's a very helpful tool for batch cooking if you want to prep enough meals to stock the freezer for busy nights.

An electric pressure cooker also helps you multitask. On a random Wednesday evening, you can have a movie night with your family while your roast for the next two nights' dinners cooks in the kitchen. You don't even have to get up to check on it, just let it do its thing!

Slow Cooker

An equally useful kitchen tool is a slow cooker, such as a Crock-Pot. You can throw a few things into the slow cooker in the morning and come home from work to a house full of delicious smells and a hot, home-cooked meal. Make enough for leftovers and let it serve double duty.

Meal Prep Techniques: Hands-On Cooking Methods

Unlike the hands-off cooking methods that don't require being check on, stirred, or peeked at until the cooking is finished, these hands-on methods require a bit of babysitting. They are not too labor-intensive, and if you're home anyway, it's really no trouble to check on a beef stew that's braising in a Dutch oven on the stovetop. Alternatively, sheet pan dinners need to be watched, but they're quick and easy enough to throw together for a weeknight dinner, usually requiring less than 30 minutes.

Dutch Oven

The beauty of a Dutch oven is that it can go from searing on the stovetop to braising in the oven and then to serving at the table. Dutch ovens come in very handy for when you want to do a classic roasting technique and you know you'll be at home anyway so it doesn't matter if you have to check on a roast chicken in the oven every so often.

Sheet Pan Meals

We absolutely love sheet pan meals! The idea is to pair protein and vegetables for a balanced meal that's cooked together on one sheet pan. You can add different herbs, spices, sauces, fats, etc., and use different meats and veggies to keep the flavors exciting. The best part is, depending on what kind of protein you're using, these types of meals usually cook in less than 30 minutes from start to finish, making them a great option for a weeknight meal even if you didn't have time to prep in advance.

Keto Batch Cooking

Cook in bulk so you can cook once and eat twice (or more) during the week. Take a roast chicken, for example—if you make roast chicken dinner with all the fixings every Sunday, just roast an extra chicken alongside. You can make it into chicken noodle soup for dinner another night and chicken salad for lunches at work. It doesn't take any longer to cook two roast chickens than it takes to cook one!

Here are a few things we like to make a big batch of to repurpose leftovers into different meals throughout the week:

- Beef pot roast: remake into tacos, beef stew, beef Stroganoff, etc.
- Roast chicken: make into creamy chicken soup, cheesy chicken broccoli casserole, BBQ chicken salad, etc.
- Baked white fish: use for fish tacos, fish chowder, etc.

- Grilled chicken or grilled steak: make into sandwiches, salads, casseroles, tacos, soups, etc.
- Roasted lower-carb produce, such as zucchini, eggplant, bell peppers, cauliflower, Brussels sprouts, broccoli, etc: roasted veggies make a great side dish for just about anything. You can also easily make them into a quiche or frittata, add them to pasta along with grated Parmesan cheese, use them as pizza toppings, and add them to sandwiches, wraps, and/or soups.

Now the question is when to find the time to batch cook. If you can do it the same day you do your big grocery haul and ingredient prep, it's one less thing to worry about doing on another day. The downside of this is that your shopping day will become a marathon of shopping, meal prepping, and cooking. If you have two days off in a row, you can do the batch cooking on your second day off. Or you can take one or two days a month and batch cook to fill your freezer so you have to do it less often. Alternatively, if you use a hands-off cooking method, you can cook a roast during a weekday while you're at work (for example, using a slow cooker) or cook a turkey on a weeknight evening in a fraction of the time (for example, using an electric pressure cooker).

Keto on a Budget

Many people think eating keto is expensive, but that just isn't the case. You can definitely eat keto on a budget! It's better if you're eating higher-quality fats and meats, but if you can't fit this into your budget, then conventional fats and meats as part of a ketogenic lifestyle are still a better option than the Standard American Diet (SAD).

Buying in Bulk

One of the easiest things you can buy in bulk are healthy fats, such as organic extra-virgin coconut oil, extra-virgin olive oil, avocado oil, grass-fed butter, ghee, tallow, and lard. Buying in larger quantities will help save money per serving. For example, coconut oil has a shelf life of around two years, so buying in bulk will save you a lot compared to buying smaller containers whenever you run out. Try to buy coconut oil and other fats in glass bottles, and if you can't, transfer them into glass containers like mason jars when you get home. This way, you'll make sure that your fats won't absorb any plastic even if the plastic is already BPA-free. Store your fats in a cool, dark place to extend their shelf life and make them less likely to go rancid.

Wholesale Memberships

Getting a membership to places like Costco, Sam's Club, or BJ's is a great way to save money, even if you'll have to pay a membership club premium. You can split a membership with friends or family, and then make a day out of it and go together once a month to buy groceries in bulk! And if your friends and family have memberships to different places, you'll be able to find the best deals for the best-quality products. For example, BJ's has the biggest variety of organic fruits and vegetables, as well as higher-quality meat. On the other hand, Sam's Club and Costco have a bigger variety of foods in general.

Shop at Farmer's Markets

If you live in a rural area, you may be able to find non-starchy vegetables at local farmer's markets. If you ask the farmers, you might find that while many of the farms aren't certified USDA organic, their produce is still grown organically. This way, you can get organically grown vegetables that are usually a lot cheaper than organic vegetables at a grocery store; they might sometimes be even cheaper than the conventional vegetables sold there! And the bonus is you'll be supporting your local farmers. Another option is to buy a share in a co-op farm so you can get good-quality produce from local farms at a lower cost than from supermarkets.

Buy Frozen Fruit and Vegetables

You can buy frozen organic or frozen conventional fruits and vegetables from the grocery store. Make sure they don't contain any added preservatives, sweeteners, or color enhancers. The ingredient list should just read one item—and that should be whatever fruit or vegetable you are buying.

Split a Cow, Pig, or Lamb with Friends and Family

Another option to save money while buying good-quality meat is to buy a whole/half/quarter of a cow, pig, or lamb at a butcher or farm with friends or family. Look for grass-fed organic beef or pasture-raised pig, and you'll frequently get it for the price of conventional meats at the grocery store. EatWild.com is a great way to find local farms that will deliver fresh produce, high-quality meat, and dairy right to your door.

Eat and Shop Local

This can include shopping at local farmers' markets, looking for local ranches/

butchers, and, if you live buy the water, shopping at local seafood markets, where you'll often be able to buy fresh seafood the same day it was caught, and usually at a better price point than if you were to buy it from a grocery store. You may have to make an additional stop to grocery shop for the week, but these options are worth the effort if you're looking to save money.

Eat Seasonally

Have you noticed that when fruit and vegetables grown in your local area go out of season they tend to double or triple in price? Where we live in Florida, berries, avocados, and oranges are our main fruit crops and the prices fluctuate drastically depending on the seasons. For example, we can find strawberries as low as $0.75 per pint when in season, but out of season their price goes up to $3.99. A way to save money is to stock up on fruit and vegetables when they are in season and either flash freeze or can them so you can enjoy them in later months without having to pay the higher prices.

Shop the Sales

If you live close to a bunch of different grocery stores, it never hurts to look at their sales fliers. When meat goes buy-one-get-one free, stock up on them and put a bunch in the freezer for later in the month or year. Additionally, you can shop at discount supermarkets like Aldi's, Big Lots, and Save-A-Lot. You might not be able to find the best quality foods, but they are cheaper than produce found in stores like Whole Foods.

How a Ketogenic Diet Can Save You Money

Since a ketogenic diet is high in fat— around 70 to 80 percent—and fat has more

than two times as many calories as protein and carbohydrates, you'll actually be saving money by eating keto because you won't be eating as much protein or carbohydrates. You'll also definitely be cutting out most of the processed foods in your diet, which are frequently more expensive because they are convenient to have on hand and require little prep or cooking. Depending on your cooking skills, eating a ketogenic diet may seem a little daunting at first, but that's nothing a little practice can't overcome!

Keto Kitchen Staples

To be able to whip up a weeknight dinner with little notice, here are a few things we like to keep stocked in our kitchens:

Pantry

- Healthy oils, such as avocado oil, EVOO, ghee, coconut oil, etc.
- Spices and dried herbs, such as garlic powder, onion powder, cumin, chili powder, paprika, Italian herb seasoning, etc.
- Shelf-stable condiments, such as Worcestershire sauce, coconut aminos, and red wine vinegar
- Seeds and nuts, such as almonds, walnuts, pecans, and sunflower seeds
- Keto sweeteners, such as liquid stevia and granulated erythritol
- Keto flours, such as almond flour and coconut flour
- And a few random items, such as coconut flakes and stevia-sweetened chocolate chips

Fridge
- Eggs
- Dairy, such as butter and cheese
- Aromatics, such as onion, garlic, and ginger
- Leafy greens and other low-carb vegetables, such as broccoli and cauliflower
- Fresh herbs
- Keto condiments, such as mayonnaise and mustard

Freezer
- Frozen berries
- Frozen meats, such as chicken thighs, ground beef, fish fillets, etc., portioned out into one-pound packages

How to Use the Freezer for Meal Prep

Take your leftovers and batch cooking methods to the next level, and stash a few meals in the freezer for super-busy nights! These dishes tend to freeze well:

- Soups, stews, curries, etc.
- Cooked roasts, like beef chuck roast and roast chicken. You can even shred the meat before freezing so it's that much easier to prepare once thawed.
- Stir-fries
- Meatballs
- Casseroles
- Ground meat–based dishes, such as taco meat
- Chopped vegetables, such as onion, carrot, celery, bell peppers, etc. The key is to pat the veggies dry, chop them, spread them out in an even layer on a large baking tray, flash freeze them, and *then* transfer them to a Ziploc plastic bag or glass container to store in the freezer.
- Sauces, such as pesto and homemade BBQ sauce. Pro Tip: freeze them in ice cube trays so you can use as much or as little as you want! Just pop them out of the tray when you want to use them.

Here are a few tips for freezer-friendly meal prep:

- Freeze things in glass or see-through plastic containers so you can see what it is (if the label gets torn off or if you forget to label something).
- Label everything with the following information: 1) what it is, 2) date it was made, and 3) reheating instructions.
- Choose containers that fit well and can be stacked in the freezer to save space. If possible, we like to use glass containers instead of plastic or foil.
- Regularly pull items from your freezer meal stash into your regular dinner rotation.
- Keep an inventory of what's stockpiled in your freezer and cross it off as you use it. Eat through the older meals first.
- Freeze some meals in individual-sized portions so you can take them for lunches

or use them for nights when you're dining alone.

- Try to remember to thaw a freezer meal the night before you want to eat it, so you're not stuck trying to microwave it the day of to get it to thaw before reheating.

Reheating Meals

When you're reheating a frozen meal, we recommend thawing it to room temperature before reheating it either in the oven or in the microwave. (Just remember to take it out of the freezer the night before!) Of course, sometimes it just isn't possible to plan ahead, and in those cases, we use the microwave to defrost.

We typically reheat multiple servings (such as a large casserole) in an oven preheated to 350°F until hot throughout. You can cover a casserole with foil to prevent it from drying out in the oven, and then remove the foil during the last few minutes or run it under the broiler to brown the top.

If we're just heating up a single serving of something (for example, a weekday lunch), we typically opt for the convenience of the microwave or a countertop toaster oven.

To reheat soup, we thaw it to room temperature, and then reheat until simmering on the stovetop.

12-WEEK MENU PLAN

While we have categorized these recipes under different headings like breakfast, lunch, dinner, snack/fat bomb, and dessert, note that certain recipes can be switched around and used interchangeably with other meals of the day if they have similar macros. To locate the exact page for each recipe, reference the Recipe List on page 163.

Week 1

	MONDAY	TUESDAY	WEDNESDAY	THURSDAY	FRIDAY	SATURDAY	SUNDAY
BREAKFAST	3 Broccoli Cheddar Egg Cups	Chocolate Coconut Almond Trail Mix	3 Broccoli Cheddar Egg Cups	Chocolate Coconut Almond Trail Mix	3 Broccoli Cheddar Egg Cups	Chocolate Coconut Almond Trail Mix	3 Broccoli Cheddar Egg Cups
LUNCH	Beanless Chili	Baked Lemon Pepper Cod with Green Beans Amandine Sheet Pan Dinner	Beanless Chili	Baked Lemon Pepper Cod with Green Beans Amandine Sheet Pan Dinner	Beanless Chili	Cheddar-Smothered BBQ Shredded Chicken with Jicama Fries	Beanless Chili
DINNER	Baked Lemon Pepper Cod with Green Beans Amandine Sheet Pan Dinner	Beanless Chili	Baked Lemon Pepper Cod with Green Beans Amandine Sheet Pan Dinner	Beanless Chili	Cheddar-Smothered BBQ Shredded Chicken with Jicama Fries	Beanless Chili	Cheddar-Smothered BBQ Shredded Chicken with Jicama Fries
SNACK / FAT BOMB	2 Toasted Coconut Vanilla Fat Bombs	Fatty Earl Grey Tea	2 Toasted Coconut Vanilla Fat Bombs	Fatty Earl Grey Tea	2 Toasted Coconut Vanilla Fat Bombs	Fatty Earl Grey Tea	2 Toasted Coconut Vanilla Fat Bombs
DESSERT	1 Almond Butter Chocolate Chunk Cookie	2 Almond Butter Chocolate Chunk Cookies	1 Almond Butter Chocolate Chunk Cookie	2 Almond Butter Chocolate Chunk Cookies	1 Almond Butter Chocolate Chunk Cookie	2 Almond Butter Chocolate Chunk Cookies	1 Almond Butter Chocolate Chunk Cookie
MACROS	1613 kcals, 20.3 g net carbs, 126.6 g fat, 87.8 g protein	1548 kcals, 21.9 g net carbs, 127.9 g fat, 73.3 g protein	1613 kcals, 20.3 g net carbs, 126.6 g fat, 87.8 g protein	1548 kcals, 21.9 g net carbs, 127.9 g fat, 73.3 g protein	1592 kcals, 18.6 g net carbs, 127 g fat, 86.9 g protein	1527 kcals, 20.2 g net carbs, 128.3 g fat, 72.4 g protein	1592 kcals, 18.6 g net carbs, 127 g fat, 86.9 g protein

Week 2

	MONDAY	TUESDAY	WEDNESDAY	THURSDAY	FRIDAY	SATURDAY	SUNDAY
BREAKFAST	Chocolate Coconut Almond Trail Mix	Blackberry Lemon Chia Pudding	Chocolate Coconut Almond Trail Mix	Blackberry Lemon Chia Pudding + Candied Spiced Pecans	Chocolate Coconut Almond Trail Mix	Zucchini Breakfast Hash	Zucchini Breakfast Hash
LUNCH	Cheddar-Smothered BBQ Shredded Chicken with Jicama Fries	Deli Turkey and Cheese Roll-Ups	Carnitas Cauliflower Rice Bowls with Guacamole and Sour Cream	Deli Turkey and Cheese Roll-Ups + Furikake Avocado	Carnitas Cauliflower Rice Bowls with Guacamole and Sour Cream	Pan-Seared Pork Chops with Creamy Pan Gravy and Garlicky Green Beans	Crack Chicken on a Bed of Spinach
DINNER	Carnitas Cauliflower Rice Bowls with Guacamole and Sour Cream	Pan-Seared Pork Chops with Creamy Pan Gravy and Garlicky Green Beans	Pan-Seared Pork Chops with Creamy Pan Gravy and Garlicky Green Beans	Carnitas Cauliflower Rice Bowls with Guacamole and Sour Cream	Pan-Seared Pork Chops with Creamy Pan Gravy and Garlicky Green Beans	Crack Chicken on a Bed of Spinach	Mushroom Swiss Burger
SNACK / FAT BOMB	2 Toasted Coconut Vanilla Fat Bombs	Brownie in a Mug	2 Toasted Coconut Vanilla Fat Bombs	Fatty Bone Broth	Candied Spiced Pecans	Candied Spiced Pecans	Candied Spiced Pecans
DESSERT	Brownie in a Mug	1 Chocolate Avocado Ice Cream Pop	1 Chocolate Avocado Ice Cream Pop	Brownie in a Mug	2 Chocolate Avocado Ice Cream Pop	1 Chocolate Avocado Ice Cream Pop	Chocolate Coconut Almond Trail Mix
MACROS	1501 kcals, 21.4 g net carbs, 121.7 g fat, 69.8 g protein	1596 kcals, 18.1 g net carbs, 111.4 g fat, 106.6 g protein	1611 kcals, 19.8 g net carbs, 130.2 g fat, 78.2 g protein	1636 kcals, 20.5 g net carbs, 127.9 g fat, 80.2 g protein	1583 kcals, 21.8 g net carbs, 125.7 g fat, 81.5 g protein	1649 kcals, 17.4 g net carbs, 118.6 g fat, 119.7 g protein	1674 kcals, 16.6 g net carbs, 126.6 g fat, 110 g protein

Week 3

	MONDAY	TUESDAY	WEDNESDAY	THURSDAY	FRIDAY	SATURDAY	SUNDAY
BREAKFAST	Zucchini Breakfast Hash	Zucchini Breakfast Hash	Protein Waffles	Protein Waffles	Protein Waffles	Protein Waffles	Protein Waffles
LUNCH	Mushroom Swiss Burger	Crack Chicken on a Bed of Spinach	Mushroom Swiss Burger	Crack Chicken on a Bed of Spinach	Turkey Kielbasa with Sautéed Buttered Cabbage	Crack Chicken on a Bed of Spinach	Sheet Pan Butter Dill Salmon with Asparagus
DINNER	Crack Chicken on a Bed of Spinach	Mushroom Swiss Burger	Turkey Kielbasa with Sautéed Buttered Cabbage	Turkey Kielbasa with Sautéed Buttered Cabbage	Crack Chicken on a Bed of Spinach	Turkey Kielbasa with Sautéed Buttered Cabbage	Grilled Steak with Blue Cheese Butter and Steamed Broccoli
SNACK / FAT BOMB	1 Cheddar Bacon Fat Bomb	1 Cheddar Bacon Fat Bomb	2 Cheddar Bacon Fat Bombs	1 Cheddar Bacon Fat Bomb	Fatty Cinnamon-Spiced Coffee + 1 Cheddar Bacon Fat Bomb	3 Cheddar Bacon Fat Bombs	1 Cheddar Bacon Fat Bomb
DESSERT	Chocolate Mint Milkshake	2 Chocolate Avocado Ice Cream Pops	1 Salted Peanut Butter Cup	2 Salted Peanut Butter Cups	2 Chocolate Avocado Ice Cream Pops	Strawberry Milkshake	1 Salted Peanut Butter Cup
MACROS	1619 kcals, 17.2 g net carbs, 119.4 g fat, 111.1 g protein	1544 kcals, 16.6 g net carbs, 112 g fat, 110.7 g protein	1526 kcals, 20 g net carbs, 120.6 g fat, 87.6 g protein	1596 kcals, 25.8 g net carbs, 126.3 g fat, 89.4 g protein	1511 kcals, 18.8 g net carbs, 120.6 g fat, 81.4 g protein	1606 kcals, 27.7 g net carbs, 122.1 g fat, 92.3 g protein	1532 kcals, 14.8 g net carbs, 131.3 g fat, 90 g protein

Week 4

	MONDAY	TUESDAY	WEDNESDAY	THURSDAY	FRIDAY	SATURDAY	SUNDAY
BREAKFAST	2 Banana Nut Breakfast Cookies	Fatty Cinnamon-Spiced Coffee	2 Banana Nut Breakfast Cookies	Kale, Sausage, and Cheese Frittata	2 Banana Nut Breakfast Cookies	Kale, Sausage, and Cheese Frittata	2 Banana Nut Breakfast Cookies
LUNCH	Grilled Steak with Blue Cheese Butter and Steamed Broccoli	Sheet Pan Butter Dill Salmon with Asparagus	Grilled Steak with Blue Cheese Butter and Steamed Broccoli	Chicken Caesar Lettuce Wraps	Mozzarella Pepperoni Tomato Basil Skewers	Chicken Caesar Lettuce Wraps	Mozzarella Pepperoni Tomato Basil Skewers
DINNER	Sheet Pan Butter Dill Salmon with Asparagus	Grilled Steak with Blue Cheese Butter and Steamed Broccoli	Sheet Pan Butter Dill Salmon with Asparagus	Mozzarella Pepperoni Tomato Basil Skewers	Chicken Caesar Lettuce Wraps	Mozzarella Pepperoni Tomato Basil Skewers	Chicken Caesar Lettuce Wraps
SNACK / FAT BOMB				Lemon Coconut Smoothie			Fatty Matcha
DESSERT	1 Salted Peanut Butter Cup	Strawberry Milkshake	1 Salted Peanut Butter Cup	1 Chewy Chocolate Chip Cookie	2 Chewy Chocolate Chip Cookies	2 Chewy Chocolate Chip Cookies	Brownie in a Mug
MACROS	1548 kcals, 13.4 g net carbs, 135.9 g fat, 84.3 g protein	1525 kcals, 15.5 g net carbs, 135.9 g fat, 74.4 g protein	1548 kcals, 13.4 g net carbs, 135.9 g fat, 84.3 g protein	1586 kcals, 14.8 g net carbs, 124.9 g fat, 95.5 g protein	1631 kcals, 14.2 g net carbs, 136.8 g fat, 82.8 g protein	1644 kcals, 14.8 g net carbs, 132.2 g fat, 98.7 g protein	1643 kcals, 12.7 g net carbs, 135.9 g fat, 83.4 g protein

Week 5

	MONDAY	TUESDAY	WEDNESDAY	THURSDAY	FRIDAY	SATURDAY	SUNDAY
BREAKFAST	Kale, Sausage, and Cheese Frittata	Kale, Sausage, and Cheese Frittata	Toasted Coconut Chia Pudding	Toasted Coconut Chia Pudding	Toasted Coconut Chia Pudding	Toasted Coconut Chia Pudding	Toasted Coconut Chia Pudding
LUNCH	Deli Meat Turkey Melt with Side Salad	Bunless Philly Cheesesteak with Sautéed Onions and Bell Peppers	Deli Meat Turkey Melt with Side Salad	Bunless Philly Cheesesteak with Sautéed Onions and Bell Peppers	Steak Fajitas with Collard Green Wraps	Roast Chicken Dinner with Mashed Cauliflower and Roasted Brussels Sprouts	Steak Fajitas with Collard Green Wraps
DINNER	Bunless Philly Cheesesteak with Sautéed Onions and Bell Peppers	Deli Meat Turkey Melt with Side Salad	Bunless Philly Cheesesteak with Sautéed Onions and Bell Peppers	Deli Meat Turkey Melt with Side Salad	Roast Chicken Dinner with Mashed Cauliflower and Roasted Brussels Sprouts	Steak Fajitas with Collard Green Wraps	Roast Chicken Dinner with Mashed Cauliflower and Roasted Brussels Sprouts
SNACK / FAT BOMB	3 Cinnamon Roll Fat Bombs	Pimento Cheese Stuffed Celery	3 Cinnamon Roll Fat Bombs	Pimento Cheese Stuffed Celery	1 Cinnamon Roll Fat Bomb	Pimento Cheese Stuffed Celery	1 Cinnamon Roll Fat Bomb
DESSERT	Coconut Hazelnut Espresso Chocolate Bark	Lemon Coconut Smoothie	Coconut Hazelnut Espresso Chocolate Bark	2 Cinnamon Roll Fat Bombs	Coconut Hazelnut Espresso Chocolate Bark	Chocolate Mint Milkshake	Coconut Hazelnut Espresso Chocolate Bark
MACROS	1511 kcals, 20.3 g net carbs, 127.1 g fat, 81.4 g protein	1517 kcals, 17.6 g net carbs, 125.2 g fat, 80.7 g protein	1481 kcals, 20.3 g net carbs, 130.2 g fat, 62.4 g protein	1572 kcals, 17.4 g net carbs, 138.2 g fat, 65.7 g protein	1483 kcals, 24.6 g net carbs, 119.6 g fat, 71.1 g protein	1585 kcals, 22.6 g net carbs, 128.5 g fat, 72.4 g protein	1483 kcals, 24.6 g net carbs, 119.6 g fat, 71.1 g protein

Week 6

	MONDAY	TUESDAY	WEDNESDAY	THURSDAY	FRIDAY	SATURDAY	SUNDAY
BREAKFAST	Toasted Coconut Chia Pudding	3 Southwestern Breakfast Egg Cups	Crunchy Cinammon Granola	3 Southwestern Breakfast Egg Cups	Crunchy Cinammon Granola	3 Southwestern Breakfast Egg Cups	Crunchy Cinammon Granola
LUNCH	Steak Fajitas with Collard Green Wraps	Roast Chicken Dinner with Mashed Cauliflower and Roasted Brussels Sprouts	Tuna Melt Casserole with Carrot and Celery Dippers	Creamy Tuscan Turkey Sausage and Spinach Soup	Tuna Melt Casserole with Carrot and Celery Dippers	Creamy Tuscan Turkey Sausage and Spinach Soup	Meatloaf Florentine with Steamed Broccoli
DINNER	Roast Chicken Dinner with Mashed Cauliflower and Roasted Brussels Sprouts	Tuna Melt Casserole with Carrot and Celery Dippers	Roast Chicken Dinner with Mashed Cauliflower and Roasted Brussels Sprouts	Tuna Melt Casserole with Carrot and Celery Dippers	Creamy Tuscan Turkey Sausage and Spinach Soup	Meatloaf Florentine with Steamed Broccoli	Creamy Tuscan Turkey Sausage and Spinach Soup
SNACK / FAT BOMB	1 Cinnamon Roll Fat Bomb	Pimento Cheese Stuffed Celery	3 Southwestern Breakfast Egg Cups	1 Almond Mocha Fat Bomb	2 Almond Mocha Fat Bombs	1 Almond Mocha Fat Bomb	1 Almond Mocha Fat Bomb
DESSERT	Coconut Hazelnut Espresso Chocolate Bark	1 Almond Mocha Fat Bomb	Coconut Hazelnut Espresso Chocolate Bark	1 Blueberry Cheesecake Cup	1 Blueberry Cheesecake Cup	1 Blueberry Cheesecake Cup	1 Blueberry Cheesecake Cup
MACROS	1483 kcals, 24.6 g net carbs, 119.6 g fat, 71.1 g protein	1618 kcals, 16.8 g net carbs, 127.6 g fat, 92.6 g protein	1548 kcals, 20.4 g net carbs, 121.4 g fat, 89.7 g protein	1550 kcals, 20.1 g net carbs, 122.4 g fat, 86 g protein	1595 kcals, 23.4 g net carbs, 132.6 g fat, 70.6 g protein	1613 kcals, 22.8 g net carbs, 123.4 g fat, 96 g protein	1546 kcals, 24.9 g net carbs, 122.9 g fat, 78.4 g protein

Week 7

	MONDAY	TUESDAY	WEDNESDAY	THURSDAY	FRIDAY	SATURDAY	SUNDAY
BREAKFAST	Fatty Cinnamon-Spiced Coffee	Crunchy Cinammon Granola	Fatty Cinnamon-Spiced Coffee	Crunchy Cinammon Granola	Fatty Cinnamon-Spiced Coffee	Crunchy Cinammon Granola + 2 Fried Hard-Boiled Eggs	Fatty Cinnamon-Spiced Coffee + 2 Fried Hard-Boiled Eggs
LUNCH	Cobb Salad	Meatloaf Florentine with Steamed Broccoli	Cobb Salad	Meatloaf Florentine with Steamed Broccoli	Charcuterie and Cheese Plate	Creamy Chicken Salad with Celery and Cucumber Slices	Lettuce Wrap BLTs with Cauliflower Faux Potato Salad
DINNER	Meatloaf Florentine with Steamed Broccoli	Cobb Salad	Meatloaf Florentine with Steamed Broccoli	Cobb Salad	Creamy Chicken Salad with Celery and Cucumber Slices	Lettuce Wrap BLTs with Cauliflower Faux Potato Salad	Creamy Chicken Salad with Celery and Cucumber Slices
SNACK / FAT BOMB					Chocolate Cheesecake Mousse	1 Brownie	1 Brownie
DESSERT	Blueberry Cheesecake Cups	Blueberry Cheesecake Cups	2 Brownies	2 Brownies	2 Brownies	Chocolate Cheesecake Mousse	Chocolate Cheesecake Mousse
MACROS	1544 kcals, 17.2 g net carbs, 125.7 g fat, 79.5 g protein	1613 kcals, 21.3 g net carbs, 128.1 g fat, 87.5 g protein	1528 kcals, 14.6 g net carbs, 123.4 g fat, 83.4 g protein	1597 kcals, 18.6 g net carbs, 125.8 g fat, 89.6 g protein	1490 kcals, 16 g net carbs, 131.9 g fat, 57.1 protein	1623 kcals, 19.7 g net carbs, 142.1 g fat, 61.4 g protein	1554 kcals, 15.7 g net carbs, 139.8 g fat, 55.2 g protein

Week 8

	MONDAY	TUESDAY	WEDNESDAY	THURSDAY	FRIDAY	SATURDAY	SUNDAY
BREAKFAST	3 Broccoli Cheddar Egg Cups	Blackberry Lemon Chia Pudding + 2 Fried Hard-Boiled Eggs	3 Broccoli Cheddar Egg Cups	Blackberry Lemon Chia Pudding + 2 Fried Hard-Boiled Eggs	3 Broccoli Cheddar Egg Cups	Fatty Earl Grey Tea	3 Broccoli Cheddar Egg Cups
LUNCH	Shredded Beef Taco Salad Bowls	Lettuce Wrap BLTs with Cauliflower Faux Potato Salad	Shredded Beef Taco Salad Bowls	Lettuce Wrap BLTs with Cauliflower Faux Potato Salad	Chicken Noodle Soup	Mozzarella-Smothered Meatballs with Zoodles	Chicken Noodle Soup
DINNER	Lettuce Wrap BLTs with Cauliflower Faux Potato Salad	Shredded Beef Taco Salad Bowls	Lettuce Wrap BLTs with Cauliflower Faux Potato Salad	Shredded Beef Taco Salad Bowls	Mozzarella-Smothered Meatballs with Zoodles	Chicken Noodle Soup	Mozzarella-Smothered Meatballs with Zoodles
SNACK / FAT BOMB	1 Brownie	1 Brownie	1 Brownie	1 Brownie	2 Savory Goat Cheese, Chive, and Pistachio Balls	2 Savory Goat Cheese, Chive, and Pistachio Balls	2 Savory Goat Cheese, Chive, and Pistachio Balls
DESSERT	Chocolate Cheesecake Mousse	Chocolate Cheesecake Mousse	Chocolate Cheesecake Mousse	Chocolate Cheesecake Mousse	Lemon Coconut Smoothie	Chocolate Mint Milkshake	Lemon Coconut Smoothie
MACROS	1520 kcals, 23.7 g net carbs, 126.2 g fat, 67.1 g protein	1582 kcals, 24.9 g net carbs, 129.6 g fat, 62.1 g protein	1520 kcals, 23.7 g net carbs, 126.2 g fat, 67.1 g protein	1582 kcals, 24.9 g net carbs, 129.6 g fat, 62.1 g protein	1628 kcals, 23.6 g net carbs, 116.7 g fat, 108.8 g protein	1542 kcals, 20.4 g net carbs, 122 g fat, 86.3 g protein	1628 kcals, 23.6 g net carbs, 116.7 g fat, 108.8 g protein

Week 9

	MONDAY	TUESDAY	WEDNESDAY	THURSDAY	FRIDAY	SATURDAY	SUNDAY
BREAKFAST	3 Banana Nut Breakfast Cookies	3 Banana Nut Breakfast Cookies	3 Banana Nut Breakfast Cookies	3 Banana Nut Breakfast Cookies	3 Banana Nut Breakfast Cookies	Protein Waffles + 2 Fried Hard-Boiled Eggs	Protein Waffles
LUNCH	Mozzarella-Smothered Meatballs with Zoodles	Chicken Noodle Soup	Grilled Steak with Blue Cheese Butter and Steamed Broccoli	Turkey Kielbasa with Sautéed Buttered Cabbage	Grilled Steak with Blue Cheese Butter and Steamed Broccoli	Turkey Kielbasa with Sautéed Buttered Cabbage	Sheet Pan Butter Dill Salmon with Asparagus
DINNER	Chicken Noodle Soup	Grilled Steak with Blue Cheese Butter and Steamed Broccoli	Chicken Noodle Soup	Grilled Steak with Blue Cheese Butter and Steamed Broccoli	Turkey Kielbasa with Sautéed Buttered Cabbage	Sheet Pan Butter Dill Salmon with Asparagus	Turkey Kielbasa with Sautéed Buttered Cabbage
SNACK / FAT BOMB	2 Savory Goat Cheese, Chive, and Pistachio Balls	Chocolate Peanut Butter Protein Bites	Chocolate Peanut Butter Protein Bites	Chocolate Peanut Butter Protein Bites	Chocolate Peanut Butter Protein Bites	Furikake Avocado	2 Fried Hard-Boiled Eggs
DESSERT	Raspberry Gelatin with Fresh Whipped Cream	Raspberry Gelatin with Fresh Whipped Cream	Raspberry Gelatin with Fresh Whipped Cream	Raspberry Gelatin with Fresh Whipped Cream	Raspberry Gelatin with Fresh Whipped Cream	Strawberry Milkshake	Brownie in a Mug
MACROS	1470 kcals, 20.5 g net carbs, 107 g fat, 95.8 g protein	1605 kcals, 21.1 g net carbs, 130.4 g fat, 93.2 g protein	1605 kcals, 21.1 g net carbs, 130.4 g fat, 93.2 g protein	1626 kcals, 20.1 g net carbs, 137.6 g fat, 83.8 g protein	1626 kcals, 20.1 g net carbs, 137.6 g fat, 83.8 g protein	1577 kcals, 23.2 g net carbs, 122.4 g fat, 83.8 g protein	1534 kcals, 17.1 g net carbs, 117.1 g fat, 92.9 g protein

Week 10

	MONDAY	TUESDAY	WEDNESDAY	THURSDAY	FRIDAY	SATURDAY	SUNDAY
BREAKFAST	Protein Waffles + 2 Fried Hard-Boiled Eggs	Protein Waffles	Fatty Cinnamon-Spiced Coffee	Zucchini Breakfast Hash	Zucchini Breakfast Hash	Zucchini Breakfast Hash	Zucchini Breakfast Hash
LUNCH	Thai-Style Turkey Lettuce Wraps	Sheet Pan Butter Dill Salmon with Asparagus	Thai-Style Turkey Lettuce Wraps	Pan-Seared Pork Chops with Creamy Pan Gravy and Garlicky Green Beans	Cheddar-Smothered BBQ Shredded Chicken with Jicama Fries	Pan-Seared Pork Chops with Creamy Pan Gravy and Garlicky Green Beans	Cheddar-Smothered BBQ Shredded Chicken with Jicama Fries
DINNER	Sheet Pan Butter Dill Salmon with Asparagus	Thai-Style Turkey Lettuce Wraps	Pan-Seared Pork Chops with Creamy Pan Gravy and Garlicky Green Beans	Thai-Style Turkey Lettuce Wraps	Pan-Seared Pork Chops with Creamy Pan Gravy and Garlicky Green Beans	Cheddar-Smothered BBQ Shredded Chicken with Jicama Fries	Mushroom Swiss Burgers
SNACK / FAT BOMB	2 Chocolate-Covered Brownie Bite Fat Bombs	2 Chocolate-Covered Brownie Bite Fat Bombs	3 Chocolate-Covered Brownie Bite Fat Bombs	2 Chocolate-Covered Brownie Bite Fat Bombs	1 Chocolate-Covered Brownie Bite Fat Bomb	2 Toasted Coconut Vanilla Fat Bombs	2 Toasted Coconut Vanilla Fat Bombs
DESSERT		Chocolate Mint Milkshake			Lemon Coconut Smoothie		1 Salted Chocolate Macadamia Nut Cluster
MACROS	1525 kcals, 22.8 g net carbs, 118.2 g fat, 89 g protein	1598 kcals, 27.1 g net carbs, 126.7 g fat, 82.1 g protein	1585 kcals, 25.1 g net carbs, 127.8 g fat, 81.7 g protein	1505 kcals, 25.3 g net carbs, 108.9 g fat, 100.7 g protein	1581 kcals, 22.2 g net carbs, 111.4 g fat, 112.8 g protein	1552 kcals, 15.6 g net carbs, 113.4 g fat, 108.7 g protein	1544 kcals, 15.5 g net carbs, 119.2 g fat, 97.1 g protein

Week 11

	MONDAY	TUESDAY	WEDNESDAY	THURSDAY	FRIDAY	SATURDAY	SUNDAY
BREAKFAST	Kale, Sausage, and Cheese Frittata	Kale, Sausage, and Cheese Frittata	Kale, Sausage, and Cheese Frittata	Kale, Sausage, and Cheese Frittata	Kale, Sausage, and Cheese Frittata	Kale, Sausage, and Cheese Frittata	Kale, Sausage, and Cheese Frittata + Fatty Cinnamon-Spiced Coffee
LUNCH	Cheddar-Smothered BBQ Shredded Chicken with Jicama Fries	Mushroom Swiss Burgers	Roasted Garlic Parmesan Cast-Iron Chicken Thighs with Sautéed Zucchini	Tuna Melt Casserole with Carrot and Celery Dippers	Roasted Garlic Parmesan Cast-Iron Chicken Thighs with Sautéed Zucchini	Tuna Melt Casserole with Carrot and Celery Dippers	Meatloaf Florentine with Steamed Broccoli
DINNER	Mushroom Swiss Burgers	Roasted Garlic Parmesan Cast-Iron Chicken Thighs with Sautéed Zucchini	Mushroom Swiss Burgers	Roasted Garlic Parmesan Cast-Iron Chicken Thighs with Sautéed Zucchini	Tuna Melt Casserole with Carrot and Celery Dippers	Meatloaf Florentine with Steamed Broccoli	Tuna Melt Casserole with Carrot and Celery Dippers
SNACK / FAT BOMB	2 Toasted Coconut Vanilla Fat Bombs		1 Toasted Coconut Vanilla Fat Bomb		2 Toasted Coconut Vanilla Fat Bombs	2 Toasted Coconut Vanilla Fat Bombs	
DESSERT	1 Salted Chocolate Macadamia Nut Cluster	1 Salted Chocolate Macadamia Nut Cluster		2 Salted Chocolate Macadamia Nut Clusters		1 Salted Chocolate Macadamia Nut Cluster	1 Salted Chocolate Macadamia Nut Cluster
MACROS	1529 kcals, 14.3 g net carbs, 118 g fat, 98.5 g protein	1547 kcals, 11.3 g net carbs, 120.4 g fat, 104.8 g protein	1563 kcals, 8.8 g net carbs, 122.7 g fat, 103.3 g protein	1612 kcals, 16.4 g net carbs, 130.9 g fat, 93.6 g protein	1645 kcals, 11.5 g net carbs, 135.7 g fat, 90.5 g protein	1605 kcals, 18.7 g net carbs, 127.8 g fat, 87.2 g protein	1501 kcals, 17.2 g net carbs, 119 g fat, 86.2 g protein

Week 12

	MONDAY	TUESDAY	WEDNESDAY	THURSDAY	FRIDAY	SATURDAY	SUNDAY
BREAKFAST	Toasted Coconut Chia Pudding + Fatty Cinnamon-Spiced Coffee	3 Southwestern Breakfast Egg Cups	Toasted Coconut Chia Pudding	3 Southwestern Breakfast Egg Cups	Fatty Matcha + 2 Fried Hard-Boiled Eggs	3 Southwestern Breakfast Egg Cups	Fatty Earl Grey Tea + 2 Fried Hard-Boiled Eggs
LUNCH	Meatloaf Florentine with Steamed Broccoli	Roast Chicken Dinner with Mashed Cauliflower and Roasted Brussels Sprouts	Meatloaf Florentine with Steamed Broccoli	Roast Chicken Dinner with Mashed Cauliflower and Roasted Brussels Sprouts	Carnitas Cauliflower Rice Bowls with Guacamole and Sour Cream	Roast Chicken Dinner with Mashed Cauliflower and Roasted Brussels Sprouts	Carnitas Cauliflower Rice Bowls with Guacamole and Sour Cream
DINNER	Tuna Melt Casserole with Carrot and Celery Dippers	Meatloaf Florentine with Steamed Broccoli	Roast Chicken Dinner with Mashed Cauliflower and Roasted Brussels Sprouts	Meatloaf Florentine with Steamed Broccoli	Roast Chicken Dinner with Mashed Cauliflower and Roasted Brussels Sprouts	Carnitas Cauliflower Rice Bowls with Guacamole and Sour Cream	Roast Chicken Dinner with Mashed Cauliflower and Roasted Brussels Sprouts
SNACK / FAT BOMB			Furikake Avocado		Furikake Avocado	Charcuterie and Cheese Plate	Furikake Avocado
DESSERT	2 Salted Chocolate Macadamia Nut Clusters	Chocolate Mint Mikshake	Brownie in a Mug	Brownie in a Mug	Strawberry Milkshake	Lemon Coconut Smoothie	Chocolate Mint Mikshake
MACROS	1618 kcals, 20.5 g net carbs, 136.6 g fat, 69.4 g protein	1517 kcals, 20.1 g net carbs, 112.6 g fat, 96.2 g protein	1495 kcals, 21.9 g net carbs, 111.3 g fat, 83.8 g protein	1515 kcals, 19.8 g net carbs, 108.7 g fat, 103.1 g protein	1498 kcals, 26.3 g net carbs, 119.6 g fat, 65.5 g protein	1522 kcals, 21.5 g net carbs, 111.3 g fat, 95.6 g protein	1526 kcals, 19.2 g net carbs, 127.6 g fat, 67.4 g protein

GROCERY AND SHOPPING LIST

Week 1

Produce
1½ cups broccoli florets
3 scallions
1 bunch parsley
6 large cloves garlic
6 large stalks celery
1 medium yellow onion
1 bunch cilantro
1 pound green beans
2 lemons (1 for zest and juice)
1 small jicama

Dairy
11 large eggs
¼ cup heavy whipping cream
2 tablespoons salted butter
3 tablespoons unsalted grass-fed butter
8 ounces shredded cheddar

Meat/Seafood
1 pound (450 g) 85% lean ground beef
1 pound (450 g) Italian sausage, hot or mild,
   bulk or removed from casing
4 (6 oz) cod filets
16 ounces cooked shredded chicken breast

Spices
1½ teaspoons onion powder
3¼ teaspoons salt
1⅛ teaspoons black pepper
½ teaspoon garlic powder
¼ teaspoon sweet paprika
1 tablespoon chili powder
½ tablespoon dried oregano
1 teaspoon cumin
½ teaspoon turmeric

Pantry
5 cups beef bone broth
6 ounces tomato paste
1 teaspoon Dijon mustard
3 ounces cacao butter
2½ cups unsweetened flaked coconut
5 teaspoons pure vanilla extract
1 cup creamy unsweetened almond
   butter
35 g stevia-sweetened dark chocolate, cut
   into 11 squares
¾ cup stevia-sweetened chocolate chips
1 cup raw almonds
2 tablespoons toasted sliced almonds
1 cup raw pecans
3 bags Earl Grey tea
9 drops culinary-grade orange essential oil
   (optional)
½ cup low-carb BBQ sauce

Oils
5 tablespoons avocado oil
3 tablespoons MCT oil
3 tablespoons coconut oil
2 tablespoons extra-virgin olive oil

Sweeteners
3 (1-g) packets stevia/erythritol blend
⅓ cup (48 g) Swerve Confectioners
¼ teaspoon liquid stevia + 9 drops

Week 2

Produce
1 teaspoon fresh lemon zest
1 teaspoon fresh lemon juice
2 tablespoons fresh lime juice
3 tablespoons fresh blackberries

1 small-medium onion
4 tablespoons minced red onion
2 medium zucchinis
5 cloves garlic
2 scallions
2 cups cauliflower rice
3½ Haas avocados
½ cup prepared guacamole
8 ounces baby bella mushrooms, sliced
1 pound green beans
8 cups baby spinach
2 cups shredded Romaine lettuce
8 lettuce leaves
1 teaspoon minced fresh parsley
4 tablespoons fresh cilantro leaves
2 teaspoons minced fresh rosemary

Dairy
1 large egg white
7 eggs
4 (1-oz) slices Swiss cheese
2 tablespoons heavy whipping cream
1 tablespoon unsalted butter
½ cup (2 oz/57 g) shredded cheddar
4 (1-oz) slices Swiss cheese
2 tablespoons unsalted butter
2 (8-oz/227-g) blocks cream cheese
6 tablespoons unsalted butter
2 tablespoons salted grass-fed butter
4 tablespoons sour cream

Meat/Seafood
½ pound bulk turkey sausage
4 (1-oz) slices no-sugar-added deli turkey
  breast
2 cups cooked, shredded pork butt
2 (16-oz, 2-inch-thick) bone-in pork
  chops
2 slices bacon, chopped
2 pounds (910 g) boneless, skinless chicken
  breasts
1 pound grass-fed 80% lean ground beef

Spices
3½ teaspoons salt
½ teaspoon smoked sweet paprika
1 teaspoon chili powder
1 teaspoon cumin
1 teaspoon dried oregano
1¾ teaspoons black pepper
1½ teaspoons cinnamon
¼ tsp Japanese furikake seasoning
1 tablespoon dried chives
2½ teaspoons garlic powder
1½ teaspoons onion powder
1 teaspoon crushed red pepper flakes
1 teaspoon dried dill

Pantry
½ cup chia seeds
2 teaspoons Dijon mustard
2 tablespoons apple cider vinegar
2 cups pecans
6 tablespoons almond flour
3 tablespoons golden flaxseed meal
¾ teaspoon baking powder
1 (13.5-oz) can organic unsweetened full-fat
  coconut milk
¾ cup + 2 tablespoons unsweetened cocoa
  powder
5½ teaspoons pure vanilla extract
½ teaspoon espresso extract
1½ cups chicken bone broth

Oils
3½ tablespoons avocado oil
2 tablespoons clarified butter (ghee)

Sweeteners
5 tablespoons granulated erythritol (or
  substitute with granulated Lakanto)
6 tablespoons Lakanto maple-flavored syrup
3 tablespoons Lakanto granulated sugar
  substitute
21 drops liquid stevia + ¼ tsp
½ cup Swerve Confectioners
½ teaspoon stevia glycerite

Week 3

Produce
½ medium onion, chopped
½ small head of green cabbage, chopped
1 tablespoon minced fresh dill
1 1emon
½ teaspoon fresh lemon zest
1 pound asparagus
3 tablespoons + 1 teaspoon minced fresh
   parsley
2 cups broccoli florets
1 fresh mint leaf

Dairy
3 large eggs
7 ounces heavy whipping cream
11 tablespoons unsalted butter
1 ounce blue cheese
6 ounces shredded cheddar
6 ounces cream cheese

Meat/Seafood
16 ounces turkey kielbasa, sliced into
   ¾-inch thick circles
2 (1-lb) bone-in ribeye steaks
4 (6-oz) salmon filets
3 slices bacon, crisped, patted dry, and
   finely chopped

Spices
1¾ teaspoons salt
½ teaspoon sweet paprika
⅝ teaspoon black pepper
¾ teaspoon garlic powder
½ teaspoon onion powder
1 pinch cinnamon
½ tablespoon flaky sea salt

Pantry
1 cup almond flour
4 tablespoons milled golden flaxseed
4 tablespoons unflavored whey protein
   powder
½ teaspoon psyllium husk powder

¼ + ⅛ teaspoon baking soda
1½ tablespoons apple cider vinegar
3¾ teaspoons pure vanilla extract
1 teaspoon vanilla bean paste
⅛ teaspoon almond extract
2 tablespoons natural unsweetened cocoa
   powder
¼ teaspoon pure peppermint extract
8 ounces hot, brewed coffee
¾ cup no-sugar-added creamy peanut
   butter
1 tablespoon chia seeds
350 g stevia-sweetened 70% dark chocolate,
   chopped

Oils
1 tablespoon avocado oil
1 tablespoon olive oil
1½ tablespoons coconut oil

Sweeteners
⅜ teaspoon stevia glycerite
12 tablespoons Swerve Confectioners
3 (1-g) packets granulated stevia/erythritol
   blend

Frozen
½ cup frozen sliced strawberries

Week 4

Produce
2 cups chopped kale
3 large cloves garlic
1 teaspoon minced fresh parsley
4 large leaves Romaine lettuce
8 cherry tomatoes
16 fresh basil leaves
1 teaspoon fresh lemon zest
1 tablespoon + ½ teaspoon fresh lemon
   juice

Dairy
14 large eggs

14 tablespoons unsalted butter, melted and cooled slightly
1 cup + 2.5 ounces freshly-shaved Parmesan
16 little mozzarella balls
¼ cup + 2 tablespoons heavy whipping cream

Meat/Seafood
1 pound bulk turkey sausage
16 ounces cooked and chopped chicken breast
16 slices pepperoni

Spices
½ tablespoon + 1 pinch cinnamon
1⅛ teaspoons salt
½ teaspoon black pepper
¼ teaspoon crushed red pepper flakes

Pantry
2 tablespoons unsweetened cocoa powder
2 teaspoons banana extract
¼ cup hemp seed hearts
2 tablespoons coconut flour
3 tablespoons golden flaxseed meal
½ cup chopped pecans
8 ounces hot, brewed coffee
½ cup mayo
½ teaspoon Worcestershire sauce
½ teaspoon coconut aminos
½ teaspoon Dijon mustard
1 tablespoon chia seeds
½ cup plain unsweetened almond milk
¼ cup canned unsweetened full-fat coconut milk
1 cup + 2½ tablespoons unsweetened coconut flakes
1½ teaspoons good-quality organic matcha powder
2 cups + 2 tablespoons almond flour
1 tablespoon beef gelatin
1¼ teaspoons baking powder
6¼ teaspoons pure vanilla extract

1 teaspoon blackstrap molasses
½ cup stevia-sweetened chocolate chips or chunks

Oils
1 tablespoon avocado oil
2 tablespoons coconut oil
1 tablespoon organic ghee

Sweeteners
6 tablespoons Lakanto golden granulated sweetener (monkfruit/erythritol blend)
3 packet (1-g) stevia/erythritol blend
2 tablespoons Lakanto maple-flavored syrup
7 drops liquid stevia
⅓ cup Swerve Confectioners

Frozen
½ cup frozen sliced strawberries

Week 5
Produce
4 cups chopped green leaf lettuce
½ cucumber, thinly sliced
1 medium tomato, chopped
¼ cup thinly sliced red onion
4 large collard leaves
1 small onion
1 medium green bell pepper
1 medium red bell pepper
½ avocado
¼ cup fresh cilantro leaves
1 lime
1 pound Brussels sprouts
½ medium-sized head of cauliflower
2 cloves garlic
3 teaspoons fresh lemon juice
1 bunch parsley
10 large stalks celery
1 fresh mint leaf
1 teaspoon fresh lemon zest

Dairy

4 (1-oz) slices cheddar cheese
4 ounces sliced American cheese
4 tablespoons unsalted butter
11 ounces cream cheese, at room
    temperature
1¼ cups heavy whipping cream
6 ounces freshly shredded white cheddar
6 ounces freshly shredded yellow cheddar

Meat/Seafood

8 (1-oz) slices no-sugar-added deli turkey
    breast
24 ounces leftover grilled steak, like ribeye
1 store-bought rotisserie chicken

Spices

1½ teaspoons salt
⅞ teaspoon black pepper
1 teaspoon no sugar added taco seasoning
2⅛ teaspoons cinnamon
1½ teaspoons onion powder
½ teaspoon garlic powder
1 pinch cayenne pepper

Pantry

8 tablespoons chia seeds
3¼ teaspoons pure vanilla extract
½ teaspoon pure almond extract
¼ teaspoon pure peppermint extract
¾ cup + 4½ tablespoons unsweetened
    shredded coconut
2 teaspoons red wine vinegar
½ cup raw unsalted sunflower seeds
1 cup almond flour
½ ounce cacao butter
¾ cup drained and chopped pimentos
1 cup mayo
2 (85-g) stevia-sweetened dark chocolate
    bars
2 tablespoons unsalted roasted hazelnuts
½ tablespoon cacao nibs
½ teaspoon coarse coffee grinds
½ cup plain unsweetened almond milk

¼ cup canned unsweetened full-fat coconut
    milk
2 tablespoons natural unsweetened cocoa
    powder

Oils

4 tablespoons extra-virgin olive oil
2 tablespoons avocado oil

Sweeteners

¼ teaspoon + 7 drops liquid stevia
¼ cup + ½ tablespoon Swerve
    Confectioners
⅛ teaspoon stevia glycerite
3 (1-g) packets granulated stevia/erythritol blend

Week 6

Produce

1 Roma tomato
¼ cup minced green bell pepper
2 scallions
1 tablespoon minced fresh jalapeño
1 tablespoon minced fresh cilantro
3 tablespoons minced fresh parsley
2 large stalks celery
2 medium carrots
2 medium onions
1 lemon
12 ounces baby spinach
7 large cloves garlic
4 cups steamed broccoli
1 cup fresh blueberries, plus 10 more for
    garnish (2 per serving) if desired

Dairy

12 large eggs
1¾ cups heavy whipping cream
1 cup shredded Monterey Jack cheese
4 ounces freshly-shredded yellow cheddar
3 tablespoons unsalted butter
3 ounces shredded mozzarella
½ ounce grated Parmesan
8 ounces full-fat organic grass-fed cream
    cheese

Meat/Seafood

2 slices bacon, cooked and crumbled
1 (12-oz) package organic, fully cooked
  Italian-style turkey sausage
1¾ pounds ground meatloaf meat, such as
  a mix of ground chuck, pork, and veal

Spices

2 teaspoons onion powder
2 teaspoons + 1 pinch salt
¾ teaspoon black pepper
1 teaspoon garlic powder
½ teaspoon crushed red pepper flakes,
  more or less to taste

Pantry

2 cups raw sunflower seeds
2 cups flaked coconut
4 tablespoons golden flaxseed meal
2 tablespoons chia seeds
2 (5-oz) cans tuna in water, drained
½ cup mayo
3½ cups organic chicken bone broth
¾ cup almond meal or flour
2 teaspoons Worcestershire sauce
¼ cup sugar-free tomato sauce
3 ounces cacao butter, melted
¼ cup unsweetened runny almond butter
2 tablespoons unsweetened natural cocoa
  powder
½ teaspoon expresso extract
⅛ teaspoon almond extract
2½ teaspoons pure vanilla extract
¼ teaspoon real fruit natural pectin

Oils

5 tablespoons avocado oil
2 tablespoons organic grass-fed clarified
  butter (ghee)

Sweeteners

3 packets stevia
4 tablespoons powdered erythritol

⅛ teaspoon + 4 drops stevia glycerite
2½ tablespoons erythritol

Week 7

Produce

1 avocado
½ cup minced red onion
8 cherry tomatoes
1 medium tomato
2 tablespoons + 1 teaspoon minced fresh
  parsley
6 cups Romaine lettuce + 6 large leaves
4 stalk celery
2 tablespoons fresh blackberries
½ cucumber
3 cups raw chopped cauliflower florets
½ small shallot
1 teaspoon minced fresh thyme
½ tablespoon fresh lemon juice
2 tablespoons fresh dill

Dairy

6 tablespoons unsalted
10 large hard-boiled eggs
2 ounces crumbled blue cheese
2 ounces sharp white cheddar
8 ounces full-fat organic cream cheese
1 cup heavy cream
3 large eggs

Meat/Seafood

12 ounces grilled chicken breast
20 slices bacon
1 ounce prosciutto
1 (8-oz) chicken breast

Spices

⅝ teaspoon black pepper
4 pinches cinnamon
½ teaspoon sweet paprika
1⅜ teaspoons salt
1¼ teaspoons onion powder
1¼ teaspoons garlic powder

Pantry
32 ounces hot, brewed coffee
3 tablespoons red wine vinegar
6 olives
½ ounce cornichons
2 teaspoons stone-ground mustard
15 tablespoons mayo
3 tablespoons toasted almonds
½ tablespoon Dijon mustard
2½ teaspoons pure vanilla extract
½ teaspoon baking powder
4 tablespoons stevia-sweetened chocolate chips
1½ ounces stevia-sweetened dark chocolate
½ cup unsweetened runny almond butter
⅔ cup unsweetened natural cocoa powder
½ teaspoon espresso powder dissolved in 1 teaspoon boiling water

Oils
4 tablespoons unrefined coconut oil
6 tablespoons extra-virgin olive oil
¼ cup avocado oil

Sweeteners
1½ teaspoons granulated stevia
½ cup Swerve Confectioners

Week 8
Produce
1½ cups broccoli florets
6 scallions
2 tablespoons minced fresh parsley
3 tablespoons fresh blackberries
6 cups shredded Romaine lettuce
12 cherry tomatoes
½ cup minced bell peppers
½ cup minced red onion
1 cup yellow chopped onion
4 cloves garlic
1 cup chopped carrot
1 cup chopped celery
1 cup peeled chopped turnip
8 tablespoons guacamole
4 tablespoons fresh cilantro leaves

1 lime
2 small-medium zucchinis
1 tablespoon minced fresh chives
1 tablespoon + 1 teaspoon fresh lemon zest
1 teaspoon fresh lemon juice
1 fresh mint leaf

Dairy
12 large eggs
1 cup shredded cheddar cheese
3 tablespoons unsalted butter
4 large hard-boiled eggs
12 tablespoons crumbled queso fresco
4 tablespoons grated Parmesan
4 ounces shredded mozzarella
4 ounces goat cheese
2 ounces cream cheese
1 cup heavy whipping cream

Meat/Seafood
2 cups cooked, shredded beef
1 rotisserie chicken, meat pulled off and chopped (about 3 cups chopped chicken, white and dark meat)
1 pound 85% lean ground beef

Spices
2¼ teaspoons onion powder
2¼ teaspoons salt
¾ teaspoon black pepper
1 teaspoon garlic powder
1½ teaspoons dried Italian herb seasoning

Pantry
½ cup + 3 tablespoons chia seeds
1 cup strong, hot, brewed Earl Grey tea
1 tablespoon MCT oil
3 drops culinary-grade orange essential oil
4 cups chicken bone broth
1 tablespoon dried Italian herb seasoning
½ cup almond flour
1 teaspoon Worcestershire sauce
½ cup low carb marinara sauce
⅓ cup toasted pistachios

1 cup plain unsweetened almond milk
½ cup canned unsweetened full-fat coconut milk
3¼ teaspoons pure vanilla extract
5 tablespoons unsweetened coconut flakes
2 tablespoons natural unsweetened cocoa powder
¼ teaspoon pure peppermint extract

Oils
Avocado oil, for the muffin tray
3 tablespoons organic grass-fed clarified butter (ghee)

Sweeteners
3 drops liquid stevia
¼ teaspoon liquid stevia
4 (1-g) packet granulated stevia/erythritol blend

Week 9
Produce
½ medium Haas avocado
2 teaspoons fresh lemon juice
4 fresh lemon wedges
½ teaspoon fresh lemon zest
1⅔ tablespoons minced fresh parsley leaves
2 cups broccoli florets, steamed
½ medium onion
½ small head of green cabbage
1 pound asparagus
1 tablespoon minced fresh dill

Dairy
13 tablespoons unsalted butter, room temperature
1 ounce blue cheese
6 large eggs
4 large hard-boiled eggs
1 cup heavy whipping cream

Meat/Seafood
2 (1-lb) bone-in ribeye steaks
4 (6-oz) salmon filets

16 ounces turkey kielbasa, sliced into ¾-inch-thick circles

Spices
¼ teaspoon onion powder
½ tablespoon cinnamon
2½ teaspoons salt
½ teaspoon sweet paprika
¾ teaspoon black pepper
¼ teaspoon Japanese furikake seasoning

Pantry
2 teaspoons banana extract
1 tablespoon + ½ teaspoon pure vanilla extract
1 teaspoon vanilla bean paste
⅛ teaspoon almond extract
1 cup unsweetened coconut flakes
1½ cups + 2 tablespoons almond flour
¼ cup hemp seed hearts
2 tablespoons coconut flour
½ cup chopped pecans
7 tablespoons milled golden flaxseed
8 tablespoons unflavored whey protein powder
½ teaspoon psyllium husk powder
½ + ⅛ teaspoon baking soda
1½ tablespoons apple cider vinegar
6 tablespoons creamy unsweetened peanut butter
6 tablespoons stevia-sweetened chocolate chips
2 tablespoons unflavored beef gelatin
2 tablespoons unsweetened cocoa powder

Oils
1 tablespoon avocado oil
1 tablespoon olive oil

Sweeteners
8 tablespoons Lakanto golden granulated sweetener (monkfruit/erythritol blend)
4 tablespoons Swerve Confectioners
¾ teaspoon stevia glycerite

1 (1-g) packet stevia/erythritol blend
2 tablespoons Lakanto maple-flavored
  syrup
7 drops liquid stevia

Frozen
6 ounces unsweetened frozen red
  raspberries
½ cup frozen sliced strawberries

Week 10
Produce
1½ teaspoons minced fresh parsley leaves
2 small-medium onions
2 medium zucchinis
2 scallions
1 large stalk celery
9 cloves garlic
1 tablespoon fresh-grated ginger
16 large butter lettuce leaves
1 small carrot
¼ cup thinly sliced red onion
¼ cup fresh cilantro leaves
2 teaspoons minced fresh rosemary
1 pound green beans
1 small jicama
8 ounces baby bella mushrooms
1 fresh mint leaf
1 teaspoon fresh lemon zest
½ teaspoon fresh lemon juice

Dairy
11 tablespoons unsalted butter
2 large hard-boiled eggs
½ cup + 2 tablespoons heavy whipping
  cream
4 (1-oz) slices Swiss cheese
4 eggs
4 ounces shredded cheddar

Meat/Seafood
½ pound bulk turkey sausage
1 pound 85% lean ground turkey
2 (16-oz, 2-inch-thick) bone-in pork chops

16 ounces cooked chicken breast, shredded
1 pound grass-fed 80% lean ground beef

Spices
1½ teaspoons black pepper
1 pinch cinnamon
¾ teaspoon smoked sweet paprika
2¾ teaspoons salt
Crushed red pepper flakes
½ teaspoon garlic powder
¾ teaspoon onion powder
1½ teaspoons flaky sea salt

Pantry
1 cup stevia-sweetened semi-sweet
  chocolate chips
1 cup macadamia nuts
2 tablespoons white chia seeds
½ cup plain unsweetened almond milk
¼ cup canned unsweetened full-fat coconut
  milk
4½ teaspoons pure vanilla extract
8 ounces hot, brewed coffee
2 tablespoons tamari sauce
2 tablespoons rice vinegar
1 tablespoon coconut sugar
2 teaspoons chili garlic sauce
1 teaspoon fish sauce
4 tablespoons natural unsweetened cocoa
  podwer
1 cup chicken bone broth
¼ teaspoon pure peppermint extract
2 tablespoons roasted, unsalted peanuts
½ cup low-carb BBQ sauce
6 tablespoons almond flour
¼ teaspoon instant espresso powder,
  dissolved in ½ teaspoon hot water
80 grams stevia-sweetened dark chocolate
3 ounces cacao butter, melted
2½ cups unsweetened flaked coconut

Oils
6 tablespoons unrefined coconut oil
2 tablespoons clarified butter (ghee)

5½ tablespoons avocado oil

Sweeteners
4 tablespoons powdered erythritol
¼ teaspoon stevia glycerite
6 (1-g) packets stevia/erythritol blend

Week 11
Produce
2 cups chopped kale
8 large cloves garlic
4 tablespoons + 1 teaspoon minced fresh
    parsley leaves
2 small-medium zucchinis
2 large stalks celery
2 medium carrots
1 medium onion
5 ounces baby spinach
4 cups steamed broccoli, for serving

Dairy
10 large eggs, lightly beaten
1 cup grated Parmesan cheese
1 tablespoon unsalted grass-fed butter
2 tablespoons freshly-grated Parmesan
    cheese
3 tablespoons unsalted butter
4 ounces freshly-shredded yellow cheddar
3 ounces shredded mozzarella
10½ ounces grated Parmesan
2 large eggs

Meat/Seafood
1 pound bulk turkey sausage
8 medium-sized bone-in, skin-on chicken thighs
1¾ pounds ground meatloaf meat

Spices
1⅛ teaspoons black pepper
½ teaspoon crushed red pepper flakes
1 pinch cinnamon
1¼ teaspoons salt
1 teaspoon garlic powder
1 teaspoon onion powder

Pantry
8 ounces hot, brewed coffee
2 (5-oz) cans tuna in water, drained
½ cup mayo
¾ cup almond meal or flour
2 teaspoons Worcestershire sauce
¼ cup sugar-free tomato sauce

Oils
2 tablespoons avocado oil
1 tablespoon unrefined coconut oil
1 tablespoon clarified butter (ghee)

Week 12
Produce
1 Roma tomato
¼ cup minced green bell pepper
2 scallions
1 tablespoon minced fresh jalapeño
5 tablespoons minced fresh cilantro
1 teaspoon minced fresh parsley
1 pound Brussels sprouts
½ medium-sized head of cauliflower
2 cups cauliflower rice
2 cloves garlic
2 cups shredded Romaine lettuce
4 tablespoons minced red onion
1 stalk celery
1½ medium Haas avocados
½ cup prepared guacamole
3½ teaspoons fresh lemon
1 teaspoon fresh lemon zest
2 tablespoons fresh lime juice
2 fresh mint leaves
½ cup frozen sliced strawberries

Dairy
12 large eggs
4 large hard-boiled eggs
1 cup shredded Monterey Jack cheese
2 ounces sharp white cheddar
10 tablespoon unsalted butter
4 tablespoons sour cream
2 cups heavy whipping cream

Meat/Seafood

2 slices bacon, cooked and crumbled
1 store-bought rotisserie chicken
2 cups cooked, shredded pork butt
1 ounce prosciutto

Spices

3¼ teaspoons sea salt
1 pinch cinnamon
1¼ teaspoons onion powder
1 teaspoon black pepper
1 teaspoon chili powder
1 teaspoon cumin
1 teaspoon garlic powder
1 teaspoon dried oregano
¾ teaspoon Japanese furikake seasoning

Pantry

9 tablespoons Chosen Foods Organic Chia
   Seeds
6¼ teaspoons pure vanilla extract
½ teaspoon pure almond extract
½ teaspoon pure peppermint extract
1 cup unsweetened shredded coconut
8 ounces hot, brewed coffee
1½ teaspoons good-quality organic matcha
   powder

1 cup strong, hot, brewed Earl Grey Tea
3 drops culinary-grade orange essential oil
6 olives
½ ounce cornichons
8 tablespoons natural unsweetened cocoa
   powder
4 tablespoons almond flour
2 tablespoons golden flaxseed meal
½ teaspoon baking powder
½ cup plain unsweetened almond milk
¼ cup canned unsweetened full-fat coconut
   milk

Oils

2 tablespoons unrefined coconut oil
1 tablespoon organic ghee
1 tablespoon MCT oil
2 tablespoons olive oil

Sweeteners

4 tablespoons Lakanto maple-flavored
   syrup
2 tablespoons Lakanto granulated sugar
   substitute
¼ teaspoons + 17 drops liquid stevia
7 (1-g) packets granulated stevia/erythritol
   blend

BREAKFAST

Toasted Coconut Chia Pudding

YIELDS 5 SERVINGS | PREP TIME: 15 MINUTES | COOK TIME: N/A

½ cup (120 ml) heavy whipping cream

1½ cups (355 ml) water

6 tablespoons Chosen Foods Organic Chia Seeds

1 teaspoon pure vanilla extract

½ teaspoon pure almond extract or coconut extract

¼ teaspoon liquid stevia

1 pinch sea salt

½ cup unsweetened shredded coconut

¼ cup unsweetened shredded coconut, toasted, for topping

Unsweetened whipped cream, for topping (optional)

1. Combine the cream, water, chia seeds, vanilla, almond extract, stevia, salt, and ½ cup coconut in a medium bowl. Cover and refrigerate overnight, or until gelled, stirring occasionally if possible.

2. Divide the pudding among 4 individual serving glasses and sprinkle 1 tablespoon toasted coconut on top of each. If desired, top each with a dollop of unsweetened whipped cream.

3. Serve chilled, or store covered in the fridge for up to 3 days.

Blackberry Lemon Chia Pudding

YIELDS 2 SERVINGS | PREP TIME: 5 MINUTES | COOK TIME: N/A

1½ cups water

½ cup chia seeds

1 teaspoon pure vanilla extract

1 teaspoon fresh lemon zest

¼ teaspoon liquid stevia

1 pinch salt

3 tablespoons fresh blackberries

1. Stir together the water, chia seeds, vanilla, lemon zest, stevia, and salt in a medium bowl.

2. Refrigerate until gelled, about 2 hours.

3. Divide the pudding into 2 individual glasses and top with the blackberries.

4. Serve, or store covered in the fridge for up to 3 days.

90-Second Microwave Muffin

YIELDS 1 SERVING | PREP TIME: 2 MINUTES | COOK TIME: 90 SECONDS

1 large egg, beaten

2 tablespoons plain unsweetened almond milk

½ teaspoon apple cider vinegar

3 drops liquid stevia

3 tablespoons almond flour

2 tablespoons golden flaxseed meal

½ teaspoon baking powder

1 pinch salt

1. Whisk together all ingredients in a microwave-safe mug until well combined.

2. Microwave until cooked, about 1 minute and 30 seconds on high in a 1000W microwave.

3. Serve, or slice in half horizontally and toast the slices before serving.

Southwestern Breakfast Egg Cups

YIELDS 12 EGG CUPS | PREP TIME: 10 MINUTES | COOK TIME: 20 MINUTES

Avocado oil, for the muffin tray

10 large eggs

¼ cup heavy whipping cream

2 slices bacon, cooked and crumbled

1 cup shredded Monterey Jack cheese

1 Roma tomato, halved, seeded, and minced

¼ cup minced green bell pepper

2 scallions, green and white parts, thinly sliced

1 tablespoon minced fresh jalapeño

1 teaspoon onion powder

1 teaspoon salt

¼ teaspoon black pepper

1 tablespoon minced fresh cilantro

1. Preheat the oven to 400°F. Lightly spray the inside of 12 silicone muffin molds with avocado oil.

2. Beat together the eggs and cream in a large bowl. Whisk in the bacon, cheese, tomato, green bell pepper, scallions, jalapeño, onion powder, salt, and black pepper.

3. Divide the mixture between the 12 muffin wells and bake until the eggs are set, about 15 to 20 minutes.

4. Cool in the molds for 10 minutes before removing.

5. Serve warm, garnished with the fresh cilantro.

Broccoli Cheddar Egg Cups

YIELDS 12 EGG CUPS | PREP TIME: 10 MINUTES | COOK TIME: 20 MINUTES

1½ cups broccoli florets

Avocado oil, for the muffin tray

10 large eggs

¼ cup heavy whipping cream

1 cup shredded cheddar cheese

2 scallions, green and white parts, thinly sliced

1 teaspoon onion powder

1 teaspoon salt

¼ teaspoon black pepper

1 tablespoon minced fresh parsley

1. Fill a small saucepan ⅔ full with water and bring to a boil. Add the broccoli and boil 90 seconds, and then drain well. Cool.

2. Preheat the oven to 400°F; lightly spray the inside of 12 silicone muffin molds with avocado oil.

3. Beat together the eggs and cream in a large bowl. Whisk in the cheddar, scallions, onion powder, salt, and black pepper.

4. Divide the mixture between the 12 muffin wells and bake until the eggs are set, about 15 to 20 minutes.

5. Cool in the molds for 10 minutes before removing.

6. Serve warm, garnished with the fresh parsley.

Crunchy Cinammon Granola

YIELDS 4 CUPS, 12 SERVINGS | PREP TIME: 5 MINUTES | COOK TIME: 15 MINUTES

2 cups raw sunflower seeds

2 cups flaked coconut

4 tablespoons golden flaxseed meal

2 tablespoons chia seeds

½ teaspoon salt

3 packets stevia

5 tablespoons avocado oil

1. Preheat the oven to 350°F.

2. Toss together the sunflower seeds, coconut, flaxseed meal, chia seeds, salt, and stevia in a large bowl, and then stir in the avocado oil.

3. Spread the granola out onto a large baking sheet and bake until golden, about 15 minutes, tossing once halfway through.

4. Cool to room temperature, and then store in an airtight container for up to 1 month.

Zucchini Breakfast Hash

YIELDS 4 SERVINGS | PREP TIME: 10 MINUTES | COOK TIME: 10 MINUTES

1 tablespoon avocado oil or light olive oil

½ pound bulk turkey sausage

1 small-medium onion, diced

2 medium zucchinis, cut into ½-inch cubes

1 large clove garlic, minced

½ teaspoon smoked sweet paprika

½ teaspoon salt

¼ teaspoon black pepper

4 eggs, fried in 1 tablespoon avocado oil

1 scallion, green and white parts, thinly sliced

1. Heat the oil in a large skillet over medium-high heat. Add the sausage and onion to a medium saucepan over medium-high heat. Cook until browned, about 5 minutes, using a wooden spoon to break up the meat.

2. Add the zucchini, garlic, paprika, salt, and black pepper, and cook until the vegetables are tender but not mushy, about 5 minutes. Don't overstir; let the zucchini sit in the pan for a bit so it has the chance to brown a little.

3. Serve each portion of hash topped with a fried egg and sliced scallion.

Kale, Sausage, and Cheese Frittata

YIELDS 8 SERVINGS | PREP TIME: 5 MINUTES | COOK TIME: 30 MINUTES

1 tablespoon avocado oil

1 pound bulk turkey sausage

2 cups chopped kale

2 large cloves garlic, minced

¼ teaspoon black pepper

¼ teaspoon crushed red pepper flakes

10 large eggs, lightly beaten

1 cup grated Parmesan cheese, divided

1 teaspoon minced fresh parsley, for garnish

1. Preheat the oven to 350°F.

2. Heat the oil in a 12-inch cast-iron skillet over medium to medium-high heat. Once hot, add the sausage, kale, garlic, black pepper, and crushed red pepper flakes and cook until the meat is browned, about 8 minutes, stirring occasionally. Cool to room temperature.

3. Lightly beat together the eggs and ¾ cup Parmesan, and pour it into the skillet with the sausage. Sprinkle the remaining ¼ cup Parmesan on top.

4. Bake until the eggs are set, about 18 to 20 minutes. If desired, broil the top to brown it slightly. Sprinkle the parsley on top.

5. Serve warm or at room temperature.

Banana Nut Breakfast Cookies

YIELDS 18 COOKIES | PREP TIME: 30 MINUTES | COOK TIME: 15 MINUTES

2 large eggs

3 tablespoons unsalted butter, melted and cooled slightly

2 teaspoons banana extract

1 teaspoon pure vanilla extract

1 cup unsweetened coconut flakes

½ cup almond flour

5 tablespoons Lakanto golden granulated sweetener (monkfruit/erythritol blend)

¼ cup hemp seed hearts

2 tablespoons coconut flour

2 tablespoons golden flaxseed meal

½ tablespoon cinnamon

¼ + ⅛ teaspoon salt

½ cup chopped pecans

1. Preheat oven to 350°F. Line 2 large baking trays with parchment paper or Silpat liners.

2. Whisk together the eggs, butter, banana extract, and vanilla. Stir in the coconut flakes, almond flour, sweetener, hemp seed hearts, coconut flour, golden flaxseed meal, cinnamon, salt, and pecans.

3. Scoop the dough (about 1 tablespoon) into 18 balls. Arrange them on the prepared baking trays, and slightly flatten each ball of dough.

4. Bake until the cookies are golden on the bottom, about 13 to 15 minutes, rotating the trays once halfway through.

5. Store in an airtight container at room temperature for up to 10 days.

Protein Waffles

YIELDS 3 LARGE WAFFLES, 6 SERVINGS | PREP TIME: 10 MINUTES | COOK TIME: 10 MINUTES

1 cup almond flour

4 tablespoons milled golden flaxseed

4 tablespoons unflavored whey protein powder

4 tablespoons Swerve Confectioners

½ teaspoon psyllium husk powder

¼ + ⅛ teaspoon salt

¼ + ⅛ teaspoon baking soda

3 large eggs

¼ cup heavy whipping cream

1½ teaspoons apple cider vinegar

1 teaspoon pure vanilla extract

1 teaspoon vanilla bean paste

¼ teaspoon stevia glycerite

⅛ teaspoon almond extract

1. Whisk together the almond flour, milled golden flaxseed, whey protein powder, Swerve Confectioners, psyllium husk powder, salt, and baking soda in a large bowl.

2. Add the eggs, cream, vinegar, vanilla extract, vanilla bean paste, stevia glycerite, and almond extract and whisk to combine.

3. Let the batter rest for 3 minutes while you preheat your waffle iron.

4. Pour ⅓ of the batter into the hot waffle iron. The waffle is done when the waffle starts to steam, about 2 minutes. Carefully remove the waffle and repeat with the remaining waffle batter.

5. Serve, or wrap each waffle half in parchment paper and store in a Ziploc plastic bag in the freezer for up to 2 months. To serve after freezing, thaw to room temperature and then toast in a convection oven or a toaster.

LUNCH & DINNER

Beanless Chili

YIELDS 8 SERVINGS | PREP TIME: 15 MINUTES | COOK TIME: 40 MINUTES

2 tablespoons avocado oil

1 pound (450 g) 85% lean ground beef

1 pound pound (450 g) Italian sausage, hot or mild, bulk or removed from casing

6 large cloves garlic, crushed

6 large stalks celery, chopped

1 medium yellow onion, chopped

5 cups (1.18 L) beef bone broth

1 (6-oz/170-170-g) can tomato paste

1 tablespoon chili powder

½ tablespoon dried oregano

1 teaspoon cumin

½ teaspoon turmeric

¼ teaspoon black pepper

Fresh cilantro, for serving (optional)

1. Add the oil to a 5-quart pot over medium-high heat. Add the beef and sausage and cook until browned, about 6 to 8 minutes, stirring occasionally. Add the garlic and cook 1 minute more, stirring constantly.

2. Stir in the celery, onion, broth, tomato paste, chili powder, oregano, cumin, turmeric, and black pepper. Bring to a boil, and then cover the pot and turn the heat down to simmer. Simmer until the vegetables are tender, about 30 minutes.

3. Serve, garnished with fresh cilantro if desired.

Shredded Beef Taco Salad Bowls

YIELDS 1 SERVING | PREP TIME: 15 MINUTES | COOK TIME: N/A

1½ cups shredded Romaine lettuce

3 cherry tomatoes, halved

2 tablespoons minced bell peppers

2 tablespoons minced red onion

1 scallion, green and white parts, thinly sliced

3 tablespoons crumbled queso fresco

½ cup cooked, shredded beef

2 tablespoons guacamole

1 tablespoon fresh cilantro leaves

2 lime wedges, for squeezing on top

1. Arrange the lettuce in the bottom of a bowl, and then top with all remaining ingredients except the lime wedges.

2. Serve along with the lime wedges to squeeze on top.

Mushroom Swiss Burgers

YIELDS 4 SERVINGS | PREP TIME: 10 MINUTES | COOK TIME: 12 MINUTES

2 tablespoons unsalted butter

½ tablespoon avocado oil

8 ounces baby bella mushrooms, sliced

⅛ teaspoon salt

⅛ teaspoon black pepper

1 pound grass-fed 80% lean ground beef

4 (1-oz) slices Swiss cheese

8 lettuce leaves

1 teaspoon minced fresh parsley, for garnish (optional)

1. Melt the butter and oil in a large nonstick skillet over medium heat. Once the butter is melted, add the mushrooms, salt, and black pepper and cook until the mushrooms are browned, about 12 minutes, stirring occasionally.

2. While the mushrooms cook, cook the burgers. Shape the ground beef into 4 patties. Preheat a large cast-iron skillet over medium-high to high heat. Once hot, add the patties and turn the heat down to medium to medium-high. Cook the burgers for 4 minutes on each side, flipping once.

3. Once the burgers are cooked, place 1 slice of cheese on each burger. Turn off the heat, drape a piece of foil on top of the burgers, and let the cheese melt.

4. Serve each burger on a bed of 2 lettuce leaves and top with mushrooms. Garnish with parsley, if desired.

Mozzarella-Smothered Meatballs with Zoodles

YIELDS 4 SERVINGS | PREP TIME: 20 MINUTES | COOK TIME: 20 MINUTES

Meatballs

1 pound 85% lean ground beef

1 large egg

½ cup almond flour

2 tablespoons grated Parmesan

1 teaspoon Worcestershire sauce

1 teaspoon onion powder

1 teaspoon garlic powder

1½ teaspoons dried Italian herb seasoning

½ teaspoon salt

¼ teaspoon black pepper

Other

Avocado oil spray

4 ounces shredded mozzarella

2 tablespoons grated Parmesan

½ cup low-carb marinara sauce

2 small-medium zucchinis, spiralized into zoodles

1 teaspoon minced fresh parsley, for garnish

1. Preheat the oven to 400°F. Line a large baking tray with foil and spray with avocado oil.

2. Add all ingredients for the meatballs to a large bowl and mix with your hands to combine (being careful not to overmix). Form the meat into 12 meatballs and arrange them on the prepared baking tray. Lightly spray the meatballs with avocado oil.

3. Bake the meatballs until fully cooked, about 15 to 18 minutes. Sprinkle the mozzarella and grated Parmesan on top and broil until the cheese is melted (watch it, this can happen fast).

4. Warm the marinara in a medium saucepan over medium heat. Once hot, gently toss in the zoodles to coat, and cook just until they're warm throughout, about 1 minute (don't overcook or the zucchini will get mushy).

5. To serve, transfer the zoodles to a serving platter, top with the cheesy meatballs, and sprinkle the parsley on top.

Meatloaf Florentine with Steamed Broccoli

YIELDS 8 SERVINGS | PREP TIME: 15 MINUTES | COOK TIME: 30 MINUTES

3 tablespoons unsalted butter

1 medium onion, finely diced

5 ounces (142 g) baby spinach

3 large cloves garlic, crushed

1¾ pounds (795 g) ground meatloaf meat, such as a mix of ground chuck, pork, and veal

¾ cup (85 g) almond meal or flour

3 ounces (85 g or about ¾ cup) shredded mozzarella

½ ounce (15 g) grated Parmesan

2 large eggs

2 teaspoons Worcestershire sauce

½ teaspoon salt

¼ teaspoon black pepper

¼ cup (60 ml) sugar-free tomato sauce, for topping (optional)

1 tablespoon fresh chopped parsley, for garnish (optional)

4 cups steamed broccoli, for serving

1. Turn pressure cooker on, press "Sauté," and wait 2 minutes for the pot to heat up. Add the butter and onion and cook until softened, about 2 to 3 minutes, stirring occasionally. Stir in the spinach and garlic, and cook until the spinach is wilted, about 1 to 2 minutes, stirring constantly. Press "Cancel" to stop sautéing. Let the spinach mixture cool a bit.

2. Use your hands to mix together the ground meat, almond meal, mozzarella, Parmesan, eggs, Worcestershire, salt, black pepper, and cooled spinach mixture in a large bowl.

3. Lay 2 sheets of aluminum foil down onto the counter. Shape the meat mixture into a loaf and place it in the center of the foil. Wrap the foil about 1½ inches up around the sides of the meatloaf so it has its own little tray.

4. Place a metal trivet into the inner chamber of pressure cooker. Add 1 cup (240 ml) water. Place the meatloaf on top of the trivet.

5. Turn the pot on Manual, High Pressure for 28 minutes and then do a quick release.

6. Use tongs or potholders to carefully remove the meatloaf.

7. Spread the tomato sauce on top and sprinkle on the parsley, if desired.

8. Serve the meatloaf along with the steamed broccoli.

Grilled Steak with Blue Cheese Butter and Steamed Broccoli

YIELDS 4 SERVINGS | PREP TIME: 15 MINUTES | COOK TIME: 15 MINUTES

2 tablespoons unsalted butter, room temperature

1 ounce blue cheese

1 teaspoon minced fresh parsley

2 (1-lb) bone-in ribeye steaks

2 cups steamed broccoli, for serving

1. Mix together the butter, blue cheese, and parsley. Spoon the mixture onto a piece of plastic wrap, roll it into a log, and refrigerate to chill (or pop it in the freezer if you're pressed for time). When it's time to serve, cut the butter log into 4 pieces.

2. Preheat your grill. Cook the steak until it reaches your desired level of doneness, about 10 to 15 minutes.

3. Serve the steak with the blue cheese butter on top, along with steamed broccoli.

Bunless Philly Cheesesteak with Sautéed Onions and Bell Peppers

YIELDS 4 SERVINGS | PREP TIME: 10 MINUTES | COOK TIME: 10 MINUTES

1 tablespoon avocado oil, divided

½ small onion, thinly sliced

½ medium green bell pepper, thinly sliced

½ medium red bell pepper, thinly sliced

12 ounces leftover grilled steak, very thinly sliced across the grain

¼ teaspoon salt

¼ teaspoon black pepper

4 ounces sliced American cheese

1. Heat the oil in a large skillet over medium heat. Add the onion and bell peppers and cook until softened but not mushy, about 8 minutes, stirring occasionally.

2. Stir in the steak and cook until warm throughout, about 2 minutes more, stirring occasionally.

3. Stir in the salt and black pepper.

4. Turn off the heat, top with the cheese, and cover the skillet for a couple minutes so the cheese can melt.

5. Serve.

Steak Fajitas
with Collard Green Wraps

YIELDS 4 SERVINGS | PREP TIME: 15 MINUTES | COOK TIME: 15 MINUTES

4 large collard leaves

1 tablespoon avocado oil

½ small onion, thinly sliced

½ medium green bell pepper, thinly sliced

½ medium red bell pepper, thinly sliced

12 ounces leftover grilled steak, very thinly sliced across the grain

¼ teaspoon salt

¼ teaspoon black pepper

1 teaspoon no-sugar-added taco seasoning

½ avocado, thinly sliced

¼ cup fresh cilantro leaves

1 lime, cut into 4 wedges

1. Working with 1 leaf at a time, lay a collard leaf flat on a cutting board with the rib side facing up. Shave off the center rib as close to the leaf as you can with a paring knife. Repeat with the remaining 3 leaves.

2. Bring a large pot water to a boil and add ½ teaspoon salt. Once boiling add the collard leaves and cook 20 seconds. Remove with tongs and transfer to an ice bath. Once chilled, remove the leaves and pat dry.

3. Heat the oil in a large skillet over medium heat. Add the onion and bell peppers, and cook until softened but not mushy, about 8 minutes, stirring occasionally. Stir in the steak and cook until warm throughout, about 2 minutes more, stirring occasionally. Stir in the salt, black pepper, and taco seasoning.

4. To assemble, lay 1 collard leaf flat on a cutting board. Spread ¼ of the meat/vegetable mixture across the center in the bottom ⅓ of the leaf and top with ¼ of the sliced avocado and 1 tablespoon fresh cilantro leaves. Squeeze 1 lime wedge on top. Fold the bottom of the leaf up over the filling, fold over the sides, and then roll the leaf up into a wrap. Continue with the remaining 3 leaves.

5. Serve.

Chicken Caesar Lettuce Wraps

YIELDS 4 SERVINGS | PREP TIME: 10 MINUTES | COOK TIME: N/A

16 ounces chicken breast, cooked and chopped

½ cup mayo

1 large clove garlic, crushed

1 tablespoon fresh lemon juice

½ teaspoon Worcestershire sauce

½ teaspoon coconut aminos

½ teaspoon Dijon mustard

4 tablespoons fresh-grated Parmesan

¼ teaspoon black pepper

4 large leaves Romaine lettuce

½ once freshly-shaved Parmesan, for garnish

1. Stir together the chicken, mayo, garlic, lemon juice, Worcestershire, coconut aminos, Dijon, grated Parmesan, and black pepper.

2. Spoon the mixture into the Romaine leaves.

3. Top with the shaved Parmesan.

4. Serve.

Roast Chicken Dinner with Mashed Cauliflower and Roasted Brussels Sprouts

YIELDS 6 SERVINGS | PREP TIME: 20 MINUTES | COOK TIME: 20 MINUTES

Roasted Brussels Sprouts

1 pound Brussels sprouts, halved

2 tablespoons olive oil

¼ teaspoon salt

⅛ teaspoon black pepper

Mashed Cauliflower

½ medium-sized head cauliflower

2 cloves garlic, peeled

2 tablespoons unsalted butter

¼ teaspoon salt

⅛ teaspoon black pepper

Other

1 store-bought rotisserie chicken

Fresh parsley, for garnish (optional)

For the Roasted Brussels Sprouts

Preheat the oven to 425°F. Toss together the Brussels sprouts, oil, salt, and black pepper in a medium bowl; spread out evenly on a large baking sheet. Bake until golden and starting to turn crispy, about 20 minutes (no need to toss halfway through).

For the Mashed Cauliflower

Add the cauliflower and garlic cloves to a medium saucepan and cover with cold water. Bring to a boil, and then turn the heat down a bit so it doesn't boil over. Continue cooking, covered, until the cauliflower is easily mashed, about 8 minutes. Drain well. Add the cauliflower and garlic cloves, butter, salt, and black pepper to a food processor and process until smooth.

To Serve

Arrange the chicken, roasted Brussels sprouts, and mashed cauliflower on a plate; garnish with parsley if desired. Serve.

Chicken Noodle Soup

YIELDS 6 SERVINGS | PREP TIME: 15 MINUTES | COOK TIME: 30 MINUTES

3 tablespoons organic grass-fed clarified butter (ghee)

1 cup chopped onion

4 cloves garlic, minced or crushed

1 cup chopped carrot

1 cup chopped celery

1 cup peeled chopped turnip

4 cups chicken bone broth

1 tablespoon dried Italian herb seasoning

1 rotisserie chicken, white and dark meat pulled off and chopped (about 3 cups chopped chicken)

2 tablespoons chopped fresh parsley, for garnish (optional)

1. Heat the ghee in a 5-quart soup pot over medium-high heat. Add the onion and cook 1 minute, stirring constantly, and then add the garlic and cook 10 seconds, continuing to stir constantly.

2. Stir in the carrot, celery, turnip, chicken bone broth, and dried Italian herb seasoning. Bring to a boil, and then cover the pot, turn the heat down to simmer, and cook until the vegetables are softened, about 20 minutes.

3. Stir in the chicken, cover the pot, and cook 5 minutes more.

4. Serve, garnished with fresh parsley if desired.

Creamy Chicken Salad with Celery and Cucumber Slices

YIELDS 1¾ CUPS, 3 SERVINGS | PREP TIME: 10 MINUTES | COOK TIME: N/A

1 (8-oz) chicken breast, cooked and chopped

½ small shallot, minced

6 tablespoons mayo

2 tablespoons minced fresh parsley

1 teaspoon minced fresh thyme

¼ teaspoon garlic powder

¼ teaspoon sweet paprika

⅛ teaspoon salt

⅛ teaspoon black pepper

3 tablespoons toasted almond, for topping

3 large stalks celery, cut into sticks

½ cucumber, cut into rounds

1. Stir together all ingredients except the almonds, celery, and cucumber. Sprinkle the almonds on top of the chicken salad.

2. Serve the chicken salad along with the celery and cucumber for dipping.

Cheddar-Smothered BBQ Shredded Chicken with Jicama Fries

YIELDS 4 SERVINGS | PREP TIME: 15 MINUTES | COOK TIME: 45 MINUTES

Jicama Fries

1 small jicama, peeled and sliced into ¼-inch thick fries (about 2 cups sliced)

2 tablespoons avocado oil

½ teaspoon garlic powder

½ teaspoon onion powder

¼ teaspoon sweet paprika

¼ teaspoon salt

⅛ teaspoon black pepper

Chicken

16 ounces cooked chicken breast, shredded

½ cup low-carb BBQ sauce

4 ounces shredded cheddar

1 scallion, green and white parts, thinly sliced

1. For the jicama, preheat the oven to 425°F. Bring a large pot of water to a boil and add ½ teaspoon salt. Add the jicama fries, bring back up to a boil, and cook for 12 minutes. Drain well and pat dry.

2. Toss the jicama fries with the oil, garlic powder, onion powder, paprika, salt, and black pepper.

3. Spread the jicama out in an even layer on a large baking tray. Roast until golden and crisp, about 30 minutes, flipping the fries once halfway through.

4. For the chicken, combine the shredded chicken and BBQ sauce in a medium saucepan over medium heat. Once hot throughout, sprinkle on the cheddar. Turn the heat off and cover the saucepan so the cheese can melt, and then sprinkle the scallion on top.

5. Serve.

Cobb Salad

YIELDS 4 SERVINGS | PREP TIME: 20 MINUTES | COOK TIME: N/A

Salad

6 cups Romaine lettuce

12 ounces grilled chicken breast, thinly sliced across the grain

4 hard-boiled eggs

4 slices bacon, cooked and chopped

2 ounces crumbled blue cheese

1 avocado, thinly sliced

¼ cup minced red onion

8 cherry tomatoes, halved

Dressing

6 tablespoons extra-virgin olive oil

3 tablespoons red wine vinegar

¼ teaspoon salt

⅛ teaspoon black pepper

1. For the salad, spread the lettuce out on a large serving platter or in 4 individual shallow bowls. Arrange all other salad ingredients on top of the lettuce.

2. For the dressing, whisk together all ingredients.

3. Drizzle the dressing on the salad and serve immediately.

Crack Chicken on a Bed of Spinach

YIELDS 8 SERVINGS | PREP TIME: 5 MINUTES | COOK TIME: 20 MINUTES

2 slices bacon, chopped

2 pounds (910 g) boneless, skinless chicken breasts

2 (8-oz/227-g) blocks cream cheese

½ cup (120 ml) water

2 tablespoons apple cider vinegar

1 tablespoon dried chives

1½ teaspoons garlic powder

1½ teaspoons onion powder

1 teaspoon crushed red pepper flakes

1 teaspoon dried dill

¼ teaspoon salt

¼ teaspoon black pepper

½ cup (2-oz/57-g) shredded cheddar

1 scallion, green and white parts, thinly sliced

8 cups baby spinach

1. Turn pressure cooker on, press "Sauté," and wait 2 minutes for the pot to heat up. Add the chopped bacon and cook until crispy. Transfer to a plate and set aside. Press "Cancel" to stop sautéing.

2. Add the chicken, cream cheese, water, vinegar, chives, garlic powder, onion powder, crushed red pepper flakes, dill, salt, and black pepper to the pot. Turn the pot on Manual, High Pressure for 15 minutes and then do a quick release.

3. Use tongs to transfer the chicken to a large plate, shred it with 2 forks, and return it back to the pot.

4. Stir in the cheese.

5. Top with the crispy bacon and scallion, and serve on a bed of spinach.

Roasted Garlic Parmesan Cast-Iron Chicken Thighs with Sautéed Zucchini

YIELDS 4 SERVINGS | PREP TIME: 15 MINUTES | COOK TIME: 45 MINUTES

Chicken Thighs

8 medium-sized bone-in, skin-on chicken thighs

½ teaspoon salt

¼ teaspoon black pepper

1 tablespoon clarified butter (ghee)

3 cloves garlic, minced

¼ teaspoon crushed red pepper flakes

2 tablespoons freshly-grated Parmesan cheese

1 tablespoon minced fresh parsley leaves

Zucchini

1 tablespoon avocado oil

2 small-medium zucchinis, sliced into ½-inch thick circles

¼ teaspoon salt

⅛ teaspoon black pepper

For the Chicken Thighs

1. Preheat the oven to 375°F.

2. Pat the chicken dry and season it on both sides with salt and pepper.

3. Add the ghee to a large (at least 12-inch) cast-iron skillet over medium-high heat. Once hot, add 4 chicken thighs skin-side-down and cook until seared on both sides, about 5 minutes on the first side and about 3 minutes on the second side. Transfer the seared chicken to a plate and repeat with the remaining 4 thighs.

4. Nestle the seared thighs back into to the skillet (it will be tight, but they should all fit). Transfer the skillet to the oven and cook until the chicken is fully cooked, about 20 to 30 minutes. It should reach an internal temperature of 165°F and the juices should run clear.

5. Transfer the chicken to a plate and place a foil tent on top to keep it warm.

6. Place the cast-iron skillet on the stovetop over medium-low heat. Add the garlic and crushed red pepper flakes to the juice and fat in the skillet. Bring to a boil and cook 5 minutes, stirring frequently.

(Continued on next page)

7. Add the chicken back to the skillet and coat it in the garlic butter. Sprinkle the Parmesan cheese and parsley on top.

For the Zucchini

1. Heat the oil in a large nonstick skillet over medium to medium-high heat. Once hot, add the zucchini, salt, and black pepper and cook until the zucchini starts to soften but not turn mushy, about 5 to 7 minutes, stirring occasionally.

2. Serve the chicken along with the zucchini.

Carnitas Cauliflower Rice Bowls with Guacamole and Sour Cream

YIELDS 4 SERVINGS | PREP TIME: 20 MINUTES | COOK TIME: N/A

2 cups cooked, shredded pork butt, warmed

1 teaspoon chili powder

1 teaspoon cumin

1 teaspoon garlic powder

1 teaspoon dried oregano

½ teaspoon salt

¼ teaspoon black pepper

2 tablespoons fresh lime juice

2 cups cauliflower rice, warmed

2 cups shredded Romaine lettuce

½ cup prepared guacamole

4 tablespoons sour cream

4 tablespoons fresh cilantro leaves

4 tablespoons minced red onion

1. Combine the shredded pork, chili powder, cumin, garlic powder, dried oregano, salt, black pepper, and fresh lime juice in a medium bowl.

2. To assemble the Carnitas Cauliflower Rice Bowls, get out 4 bowls. In each bowl, arrange the following: ½ cup cauliflower rice, ½ cup shredded pork, and ½ cup shredded Romaine. Top each with 2 tablespoons guacamole, 1 tablespoon sour cream, 1 tablespoon cilantro leaves, and 1 tablespoon minced red onion.

3. Serve.

Pan-Seared Pork Chops with Creamy Pan Gravy and Garlicky Green Beans

YIELDS 4 SERVINGS | PREP TIME: 10 MINUTES | COOK TIME: 20 MINUTES

Pork Chops

2 (16-oz, 2-inch thick) bone-in pork chops

1 teaspoon salt

½ teaspoon black pepper

2 tablespoons clarified butter (ghee)

2 large cloves garlic, minced

2 teaspoons minced fresh rosemary

2 tablespoons heavy whipping cream

Green Beans

1 tablespoon unsalted butter

1 tablespoon avocado oil

1 pound green beans, ends trimmed and steamed until fork-tender

2 cloves garlic, thinly sliced

½ cup chicken stock

¼ teaspoon salt

¼ teaspoon black pepper

1. For the pork chops, preheat oven to 400°F.

2. Pat the pork chops dry and season on both sides with salt and pepper.

3. Heat a medium-large cast-iron skillet over medium-high heat. Add the ghee and, once melted, sear the pork chops, about 4 to 5 minutes on each side, flipping once.

4. Transfer the pan to the oven and cook until the pork chops are fully cooked (the thickest part should read 145°F on an instant-read thermometer), about 8 to 10 minutes. Transfer the pork chops to a serving plate and place a foil tent on top to keep them warm.

5. To make the gravy, place the same skillet, with the drippings, over low heat. Add the garlic and rosemary and cook until fragrant, about 2 to 4 minutes, stirring constantly. Turn off the heat and whisk in the cream.

6. For the green beans, heat a large cast-iron skillet over medium to medium-high heat. Once hot, add the butter and oil. Once the butter is melted, add the green beans, garlic, chicken stock, salt, and black pepper. Cover the skillet and cook 10 minutes, stirring occasionally. Uncover the skillet and cook until the liquid is evaporated and the beans start to brown in spots, about 5 minutes more, stirring frequently.

7. Serve the pork chops along with the gravy to drizzle on top with the green beans on the side.

Turkey Kielbasa with Sautéed Buttered Cabbage

YIELDS 4 SERVINGS | PREP TIME: 15 MINUTES | COOK TIME: 25 MINUTES

2 tablespoons unsalted butter

1 tablespoon avocado oil

16 ounces turkey kielbasa, sliced into ¾-inch thick circles

½ medium onion, chopped

½ small head green cabbage, chopped

1 tablespoon apple cider vinegar

½ teaspoon salt

½ teaspoon sweet paprika

¼ teaspoon black pepper

1 tablespoon minced fresh parsley

1. Heat the butter and oil in a 5-quart pot over medium-high heat. Once the butter is melted, add the kielbasa and cook until browned, about 8 minutes, stirring occasionally. Use a slotted spoon to transfer the kielbasa to a bowl and set aside.

2. Turn the heat down to medium, and add the onion, cabbage, vinegar, and salt. Cover and cook until the cabbage is tender, about 10 to 15 minutes, stirring occasionally.

3. Add the browned kielbasa, paprika, and black pepper and cook until the sausage is warm, about 3 minutes.

4. Sprinkle parsley on top and serve.

Lettuce Wrap BLTs
with Cauliflower Faux Potato Salad

YIELDS 6 SERVINGS | PREP TIME: 15 MINUTES | COOK TIME: 15 MINUTES

Cauliflower Faux Potato Salad

3 cups raw chopped cauliflower florets

6 tablespoons mayo

½ tablespoon fresh lemon juice

½ tablespoon Dijon mustard

1 teaspoon onion powder

1 teaspoon garlic powder

½ teaspoon salt

¼ teaspoon sweet paprika

⅛ teaspoon black pepper

¼ cup minced red onion

2 large hard-boiled eggs, chopped

2 tablespoons fresh dill

BLTs

6 large leaves Romaine lettuce

3 tablespoons mayo

12 slices bacon, crisped

1 medium tomato, thinly sliced

1. Add the cauliflower to a medium saucepan and cover with cool water by 2 inches. Bring to a boil, and then turn heat down and simmer until fork-tender, about 5 minutes. Drain and cool completely.

2. Stir together the mayo, lemon juice, Dijon, onion powder, garlic powder, salt, paprika, black pepper, red onion, eggs, and dill in a large bowl. Fold in the cauliflower to coat.

3. Chill 1 hour, or store in the fridge for up to 5 days.

4. For the BLTs, lay the lettuces leaves flat on a cutting board. On each, spread ½ tablespoon mayo, 2 slices of bacon, and ⅙ of the tomato slices.

5. Serve the BLTs along with the faux potato salad.

Thai-Style Turkey Lettuce Wraps

YIELDS 4 SERVINGS | PREP TIME: 10 MINUTES | COOK TIME: 20 MINUTES

2 tablespoons coconut oil

1 pound 85% lean ground turkey

1 small yellow onion, diced

1 large stalk celery, diced

4 cloves garlic, crushed

1 tablespoon fresh-grated ginger

2 tablespoons tamari sauce

2 tablespoons rice vinegar

1 tablespoon coconut sugar

2 teaspoons chili garlic sauce

1 teaspoon fish sauce

½ cup chicken bone broth

8 large butter lettuce leaves

1 small carrot, thinly sliced, for garnish

¼ cup thinly sliced red onion, for garnish

¼ cup fresh cilantro leaves, for garnish

2 tablespoons roasted, unsalted peanuts, for garnish

Crushed red pepper flakes, for garnish

1. Heat the oil in a large skillet over medium-high heat. Once hot, add the turkey, onion, and celery and cook until the meat is browned and the vegetables are tender, about 8 to 10 minutes, stirring occasionally.

2. Add the garlic and ginger, and cook 1 minute, stirring constantly.

3. Add the tamari sauce, vinegar, sugar, chili garlic sauce, fish sauce, and chicken bone broth. Bring to a simmer and cook, stirring frequently, until the liquid is mostly evaporated, about 10 minutes.

4. To serve, divide the meat mixture between the 8 lettuce cups. Top each with carrot, red onion, cilantro, peanuts, and crushed red pepper flakes.

Deli Meat Turkey Melt with Side Salad

YIELDS 4 SERVINGS | PREP TIME: 15 MINUTES | COOK TIME: 2 MINUTES

Turkey Melt

8 (1-oz) slices no-sugar-added deli turkey breast

4 (1-oz) slices cheddar cheese

Salad

2 tablespoons extra-virgin olive oil

2 teaspoons red wine vinegar

¼ teaspoon salt

⅛ teaspoon black pepper

4 cups chopped green leaf lettuce

½ cucumber, thinly sliced

1 medium tomato, chopped

¼ cup thinly sliced red onion

1. For the turkey melt, preheat the broiler. Fold each slice of turkey in half, and place 4 stacks of 2 slices of turkey on the tray. Top each stack with a slice of cheese. Broil until the cheese is melted (watch it, this can happen fast). Serve immediately.

2. For the salad, whisk together the oil, vinegar, salt, and black pepper in a large bowl. Toss in all the remaining vegetables to coat, and serve immediately

Creamy Tuscan Turkey Sausage and Spinach Soup

YIELDS 4 SERVINGS | PREP TIME: 10 MINUTES | COOK TIME: 15 MINUTES

2 tablespoons organic grass-fed clarified butter (ghee)

1 (12-oz/340-g) package organic, fully cooked Italian-style turkey sausage, sliced

1 medium onion, diced

4 cloves garlic, crushed

3½ cups (830 ml) organic chicken bone broth

½ teaspoon crushed red pepper flakes, more or less to taste

6 cups (255 g) organic baby spinach

½ cup (120 ml) heavy whipping cream

Sea salt, to taste

Black pepper, to taste

Fresh lemon wedges, to squeeze on top (optional)

1. Heat the ghee in a 3-quart saucepan over medium to medium-high heat. Add the sausage and onion and cook until the sausage is starting to brown and the onion is softened, about 6 to 8 minutes, stirring occasionally. Add the garlic and cook 1 minute more, stirring constantly.

2. Add the bone broth and crushed red pepper flakes and bring to a boil; cover the saucepan, turn the heat down to simmer, and cook 5 minutes.

3. Stir in the spinach and cook until wilted, stirring constantly, about 1 to 2 minutes. Turn off the heat and stir in the cream.

4. Taste and season with sea salt and black pepper as desired.

5. Serve with fresh lemon wedges to squeeze into the soup if desired.

Sheet Pan Butter Dill Salmon with Asparagus

YIELDS 4 SERVINGS | PREP TIME: 10 MINUTES | COOK TIME: 15 MINUTES

1 tablespoon olive oil

4 (6-oz) salmon filets

1 pound asparagus, woody ends trimmed off

½ teaspoon salt

¼ teaspoon black pepper

2 tablespoons butter, melted

½ teaspoon fresh lemon zest

1 tablespoon minced fresh dill

4 fresh lemon wedges

1. Preheat the oven to 425°F. Line a large baking tray with foil and drizzle on the olive oil.

2. Arrange the salmon filets and asparagus on the baking tray and season with salt and pepper.

3. Bake until the salmon is opaque and flakes easily with a fork and the asparagus is tender, about 12 to 15 minutes.

4. Transfer the salmon and asparagus to a serving platter.

5. Stir together the melted butter, lemon zest, and dill in a small bowl and drizzle on top of the salmon and asparagus.

6. Serve along with the lemon wedges to squeeze on top.

Baked Lemon Pepper Cod with Green Beans Amandine Sheet Pan Dinner

YIELDS 4 SERVINGS | PREP TIME: 15 MINUTES | COOK TIME: 15 MINUTES

Cod

4 (6-oz) cod filets

1 tablespoon extra-virgin olive oil

1 teaspoon fresh lemon zest

¼ teaspoon salt

¼ teaspoon black pepper

Green Beans

1 pound green beans, stem ends trimmed

1 tablespoon extra-virgin olive oil

¼ teaspoon salt

¼ teaspoon black pepper

Lemon Butter Sauce

2 tablespoons salted butter

2 teaspoons fresh lemon juice

1 teaspoon Dijon mustard

Other

2 tablespoons toasted sliced almonds

1 lemon, cut into wedges

1. Preheat the oven to 400°F. Line a large baking tray with parchment paper or a Silpat liner.

2. Pat the cod filets dry, and then drizzle the oil on both sides and season with the lemon zest, salt, and pepper. Place the cod filets on one half of the prepared baking tray so they're not touching.

3. Toss together the green beans, oil, salt, and pepper in a bowl, and then spread out onto the other half of the same baking tray.

4. Bake the fish and green beans until the fish is opaque and flakes easily with a fork, and the green beans are fork-tender, about 15 minutes.

5. Meanwhile, make the lemon butter sauce by melting together the butter, lemon juice, and Dijon.

6. To serve, transfer the fish and green beans to a serving platter. Sprinkle the almonds on top of the green beans. Arrange the lemon wedges next to the fish. Serve along with the lemon butter sauce to drizzle on top.

Tuna Melt Casserole
with Carrot and Celery Dippers

YIELDS 4 SERVINGS | PREP TIME: 10 MINUTES | COOK TIME: 20 MINUTES

2 (5-oz) cans tuna in water, drained

½ cup mayo

2 tablespoons minced fresh parsley

1 teaspoon garlic powder

1 teaspoon onion powder

¼ teaspoon black pepper

4 ounces freshly-shredded yellow cheddar

2 medium carrots, cut into sticks

2 large stalks celery, cut into sticks

1. Preheat the oven to 400°F.

2. Mix together the tuna, mayo, parsley, garlic powder, onion powder, and black pepper in a medium bowl. Spread the tuna mixture out into the bottom of a 9 by 5-inch loaf pan. Sprinkle the cheddar on top.

3. Bake until the casserole is warm throughout, about 15 minutes, and then broil to brown the top.

4. Serve the casserole along with carrot and celery sticks for dipping.

Dill Relish Deviled Eggs

YIELDS 24 DEVILED EGG HALVES, 6 SERVINGS | PREP TIME: 15 MINUTES | COOK TIME: N/A

12 large hard-boiled eggs

¾ cup mayo

3 tablespoons dill relish

½ teaspoon garlic powder

½ teaspoon dried dill

⅛ teaspoon salt

⅛ teaspoon black pepper

1 teaspoon minced fresh parsley
  or dill, for garnish

1. Cut the eggs in half and scoop the yolks into a medium bowl.

2. To the bowl with the yolks, add the mayo, relish, garlic powder, dried dill, salt, and black pepper. Use a handheld electric beater to mix until well-combined.

3. Pipe or spoon the yolk mixture into the whites and garnish with fresh parsley or dill.

4. Serve, or store in an airtight container in the fridge for up to 5 days.

Charcuterie and Cheese Plate

YIELDS 1 SERVING | PREP TIME: 10 MINUTES | COOK TIME: N/A

2 ounces sharp white cheddar, sliced

1 ounce prosciutto

6 olives

½ ounce cornichons

1 stalk celery, cut into sticks

Optional

2 teaspoons stone-ground mustard

2 tablespoons fresh blackberries

1. Arrange all components on a plate or in a meal prep container.

2. Serve.

SNACKS

Chocolate Peanut Butter Protein Bites

YIELDS 4 BALLS, 4 SERVINGS | PREP TIME: 10 MINUTES | COOK TIME: N/A

6 tablespoons creamy unsweetened peanut butter (the thick kind, not the super-runny stuff)

4 tablespoons flavored low-carb protein powder (we like Quest Salted Caramel Protein Powder)

6 tablespoons stevia-sweetened chocolate chips

1. Stir together the peanut butter and protein powder. Refrigerate to chill, about 15 minutes.

2. Roll the mixture into 4 balls and roll each ball in mini chocolate chips to coat.

3. Store the bites covered in the fridge for up to 2 weeks.

Salted Chocolate Macadamia Nut Clusters

YIELDS 12 SERVINGS | PREP TIME: 20 MINUTES | COOK TIME: N/A

1 cup stevia-sweetened semi-sweet chocolate chips

1 cup macadamia nuts

1½ teaspoons flaky sea salt

1. Line a large baking tray with parchment paper.

2. Melt the chocolate in the microwave or in a double boiler.

3. Stir the macadamia nuts into the chocolate.

4. Drop 1-tablespoon mounds onto the prepared tray, and sprinkle the sea salt on top.

5. Let the chocolate set, and then store covered in the fridge for up to 2 weeks.

Chocolate Peanut Butter Coconut Haystack Cookies

YIELDS 24 COOKIES, 12 SERVINGS | PREP TIME: 20 MINUTES | COOK TIME: 5 MINUTES

1 (7-g/198-oz) unsweetened shredded coconut

1 (3-oz/85-g) bar stevia-sweetened dark chocolate, chopped

3 tablespoons coconut butter

4 tablespoons unsweetened creamy peanut butter

⅛ teaspoon fine salt

1. Preheat the oven to 350°F. Spread the coconut out on a large baking sheet and bake until starting to turn light golden brown, about 4 to 6 minutes, stirring once halfway through. Remove and cool.

2. Melt the chocolate in a double boiler or microwave. Stir in the coconut butter until melted, and then stir in the peanut butter and salt.

3. Mix the coconut into the chocolate mixture and drop by the spoonful onto parchment paper-lined baking sheets.

4. Refrigerate until the haystacks are set, about 20 minutes. Store in a covered container in the fridge.

Pimento Cheese Stuffed Celery

YIELDS ABOUT 3½ CUPS, 10 SERVINGS | PREP TIME: 20 MINUTES | COOK TIME: N/A

6 ounces cream cheese, at room temperature

1 cup mayo

¼ cup heavy whipping cream

2½ teaspoons fresh lemon juice

1½ teaspoons onion powder

½ teaspoon garlic powder

¼ teaspoon black pepper

1 pinch cayenne pepper

6 ounces freshly-shredded white cheddar

6 ounces freshly-shredded yellow cheddar

¾ cup drained and finely chopped pimentos

1 tablespoon minced fresh parsley, for garnish

10 large stalks celery, for serving

1. Use a handheld electric mixer to beat together the cream cheese, mayo, heavy whipping cream, lemon juice, onion powder, garlic powder, black pepper, and cayenne pepper in a large bowl.

2. Stir in the shredded white cheddar, shredded yellow cheddar, and pimentos.

3. Transfer to a serving dish and sprinkle the parsley on top.

4. Spoon the pimento cheese into the celery sticks, or use the celery as dippers.

Deli Turkey and Cheese Roll-Ups

YIELDS 2 SERVINGS | PREP TIME: 5 MINUTES | COOK TIME: N/A

4 (1-oz) slices no-sugar-added
   deli turkey breast
4 (1-oz) slices Swiss cheese
2 teaspoons Dijon mustard

1. Lay the turkey slices down on a cutting board and place the cheese slices directly on top.

2. Spread ½ teaspoon Dijon on top of each piece of cheese, and roll each up.

3. Serve.

White Cheddar and Chive Cheese Crisps

YIELDS 16 CRISPS | PREP TIME: 2 MINUTES | COOK TIME: 8 MINUTES

1 cup pre-shredded white
   cheddar cheese
4 teaspoons dried chives

1. Preheat the oven to 400°F.

2. Put 1 tablespoon cheese into each of 16 mini muffin wells. Sprinkle the dried chives on top of the cheese.

3. Bake until golden along the outside, about 8 to 10 minutes.

4. Cool slightly, and then remove.

5. Serve.

Candied Spiced Pecans

YIELDS 2 CUPS/8 SERVINGS | PREP TIME: 5 MINUTES | COOK TIME: 30 MINUTES

1 large egg white

5 tablespoons granulated erythritol

1½ teaspoons vanilla extract

1½ teaspoons cinnamon

¼ teaspoon salt

½ tablespoon water

2 cups pecans

1. Preheat the oven to 300°F; line a large baking tray with parchment paper or a Silpat liner.

2. Whisk together the egg white, erythritol, vanilla, cinnamon, salt, and water until foamy.

3. Stir the pecans in the egg white mixture to coat.

4. Spread the nuts out in an even layer on the prepared baking sheet.

5. Bake until golden, about 25 to 30 minutes, stirring once halfway through. The nuts and their coating will harden as they cool.

6. Store in an airtight container at room temperature up to 2 weeks.

Mozzarella Pepperoni Tomato Basil Skewers

YIELDS 8 SKEWERS, 4 SERVINGS | PREP TIME: 10 MINUTES | COOK TIME: N/A

16 little mozzarella balls
16 fresh basil leaves
16 slices pepperoni
8 cherry tomatoes

1. Thread ingredients onto a small appetizer skewer in the following order: 1 little mozzarella ball, 1 basil leaf folded in half, 1 slice pepperoni folded in half, 1 cherry tomato, 1 slice pepperoni folded in half, 1 basil leaf folded in half, and 1 little mozzarella ball. Continue this way with the remaining ingredients so you end up with 8 skewers total.

2. Serve.

Fried Hard-Boiled Eggs

YIELDS 1 SERVING | PREP TIME: 1 MINUTE | COOK TIME: 4 MINUTES

1 tablespoon unsalted butter

2 large hard-boiled eggs, peeled and cut in half lengthwise

1 pinch salt

1 pinch black pepper

1 pinch onion powder (optional)

½ teaspoon minced fresh parsley leaves, for garnish

1. Melt the butter in a small nonstick skillet over medium to medium-high heat.

2. Once melted, add the egg halves and cook until golden on each side, about 2 minutes per side.

3. Season with salt and pepper. Add onion powder if desired.

4. Transfer to a plate and sprinkle on the parsley.

5. Serve.

Chocolate Coconut Almond Trail Mix

YIELDS 3¾ CUPS, 10 SERVINGS (1 SERVING EQUALS ⅓ CUP)
PREP TIME: 10 MINUTES | COOK TIME: 15 MINUTES

Coconut oil spray, for the pan

1 cup raw almonds

1 cup raw pecans

1 cup coconut flakes

2 teaspoons pure vanilla extract

¼ teaspoon liquid stevia

¼ teaspoon fine salt

¾ cup stevia-sweetened chocolate chips

1. Preheat the oven to 325°F; line a large baking tray with parchment paper and spray the top of the parchment with coconut oil spray.

2. Toss together the almonds, pecans, coconut flakes, vanilla, stevia, and salt in a large bowl.

3. Spread out on the prepared baking sheet and bake until golden, about 15 minutes.

4. Cool completely and then stir in the chocolate chips.

5. Store in an airtight container at room temperature for up to 2 weeks.

Furikake Avocado

YIELDS 1 SERVING | PREP TIME: 2 MINUTES | COOK TIME: N/A

1 squeeze fresh lemon

½ medium Haas avocado

¼ teaspoon Japanese furikake seasoning

1. Squeeze the lemon on top of the avocado and sprinkle on the furikake.

2. Serve immediately.

FAT BOMBS

Cheddar Bacon Fat Bombs

YIELDS 10 FAT BOMBS | PREP TIME: 15 MINUTES | COOK TIME: N/A

6 ounces shredded cheddar

6 ounces cream cheese, slightly softened

¾ teaspoon garlic powder

½ teaspoon onion powder

⅛ teaspoon black pepper

3 slices bacon, crisped, patted dry, and finely chopped

2 tablespoons minced fresh parsley

1. Add the cheddar, cream cheese, garlic powder, onion powder, and black pepper to a medium bowl and stir well to combine.

2. Place a piece of plastic wrap directly on top of the cheese and chill 8 minutes in the freezer.

3. Roll the cheese mixture into 10 balls.

4. Combine the bacon and parsley in a shallow bowl.

5. Roll each cheese ball in the bacon mixture to coat.

6. Serve, or store in an airtight container in the fridge for up to 1 week.

Ranch Cheese Ball Fat Bombs

YIELDS 14 CHEESE BALLS | PREP TIME: 15 MINUTES | COOK TIME: N/A

6 ounces shredded cheddar

6 ounces cream cheese, slightly softened

¾ teaspoon garlic powder

½ teaspoon dried dill

5 tablespoons finely chopped pecans

1 tablespoon minced fresh parsley

1. Add the cheddar, cream cheese, garlic powder, and dried dill to a medium bowl and stir well to combine.

2. Place a piece of plastic wrap directly on top of the cheese and chill 8 minutes in the freezer.

3. Roll the cheese mixture into 14 balls.

4. Combine the pecans and parsley in a shallow bowl.

5. Roll each cheese ball in the pecan mixture to coat.

6. Serve, or store in an airtight container in the fridge for up to 1 week.

Savory Goat Cheese, Chive, and Pistachio Balls

YIELDS 4 SERVINGS/8 CHEESE BALLS | PREP TIME: 15 MINUTES | COOK TIME: N/A

4 ounces (115 g) goat cheese

2 ounces (57 g) cream cheese

1½ tablespoons heavy whipping cream

1 tablespoon minced fresh chives

⅓ cup toasted pistachios, finely chopped

1. Beat together the goat cheese, cream cheese, cream, and chives in a medium bowl.

2. Lay a piece of plastic wrap directly on top of the cheese mixture, and refrigerate until fully chilled, about 2 hours.

3. Divide the cheese into 8 equal pieces, roll each into a ball, and roll in pistachios to coat.

4. Serve, or refrigerate up to 3 days before serving.

Almond Mocha Fat Bombs

YIELDS 7 FAT BOMBS | PREP TIME: 10 MINUTES | COOK TIME: N/A

3 ounces cacao butter, melted

¼ cup unsweetened runny almond butter

4 tablespoons powdered erythritol

2 tablespoons unsweetened natural cocoa powder

1 teaspoon pure vanilla extract

½ teaspoon expresso extract

⅛ teaspoon almond extract

⅛ teaspoon stevia glycerite

1 pinch salt

1. Stir together the melted cacao butter and almond butter until smooth. Mix in all remaining ingredients.

2. Divide the mixture into 7 fat bomb molds (each fat bomb about 2 tablespoons).

3. Refrigerate until set. Store the leftovers covered in the fridge for up to 2 weeks.

Chocolate Chip Cookie Dough Fat Bombs

YIELD 12 SERVINGS | PREP TIME: 20 MINUTES | COOK TIME: N/A

4 ounces (115 g) organic grass-fed cream cheese, at room temperature

4 tablespoons unsalted organic grass-fed butter, at room temperature

4 tablespoons unsweetened creamy almond butter

1½ tablespoons Swerve Confectioners

1 teaspoon pure vanilla extract

½ teaspoon blackstrap molasses

¼ + ⅛ teaspoon granulated stevia blend (such as Pyure Organic Stevia)

¼ teaspoon baking soda

⅛ teaspoon salt

4 tablespoons stevia-sweetened chocolate chips or chopped chocolate

1. Cream together the cream cheese and butter, and then beat in the almond butter, Swerve Confectioners, vanilla, molasses, powdered stevia, baking soda, and salt. Fold in the chocolate chips.

2. Cover and refrigerate until the dough is firm enough to scoop into balls, about 2 to 4 hours.

3. Divide into 10 equal portions, and store covered in the fridge.

Toasted Coconut Vanilla Fat Bombs

YIELDS 12 FAT BOMBS | PREP TIME: 10 MINUTES | COOK TIME: N/A

3 ounces cacao butter, melted

3 tablespoons coconut oil, melted

¾ cup unsweetened flaked coconut

¾ cup unsweetened flaked coconut, toasted

3 (1-g) packets stevia/erythrtiol blend

2 teaspoons pure vanilla extract

1 pinch salt

1. Stir together all ingredients in a medium bowl until well combined.

2. Spoon the mixture into 12 fat bomb molds.

3. Refrigerate until chilled, about 10 minutes in the freezer or 30 minutes in the fridge.

4. Store in an airtight container in the fridge for up to 2 weeks.

NOTE

Unlike most fat bombs, since this recipe uses cacao butter as the base, these will soften but not fully melt at room temperature.

Chocolate-Covered Brownie Bite Fat Bombs

YIELDS 10 FAT BOMBS | PREP TIME: 20 MINUTES | COOK TIME: N/A

6 tablespoons almond flour

4 tablespoons powdered erythritol

2 tablespoons unsweetened natural cocoa powder

1 pinch salt

1 teaspoon pure vanilla extract

¼ teaspoon instant espresso powder, dissolved in ½ teaspoon hot water

¼ teaspoon stevia glycerite

6 tablespoons unsalted butter, melted and cooled

2.8 ounces (80 g) stevia-sweetened dark chocolate

1. Whisk together the almond flour, powdered erythritol, cocoa powder, and salt in a medium bowl.

2. Stir in the vanilla, dissolved espresso powder, stevia glycerite, and melted butter.

3. Place a piece of plastic wrap directly on the dough and chill in the freezer for 15 minutes.

4. Scoop the dough into 10 fat bombs and roll each into a ball; chill in the freezer for 5 minutes.

5. Melt the stevia-sweetened dark chocolate in a microwave or double boiler, and dip each ball in the melted chocolate to coat. Let the excess chocolate drip off and place the chocolate-covered brownie bites onto a parchment paper–lined baking tray.

6. Let the chocolate harden before serving. Store covered in the fridge for up to 2 weeks.

Salted Peanut Butter Cups

¾ cup no-sugar-added creamy peanut butter (see note)

4 tablespoons unsalted butter, softened slightly

4 tablespoons Swerve Confectioners

1 teaspoon vanilla extract

⅛ teaspoon stevia glycerite

⅛ teaspoon salt

12.3 ounces (350 g) stevia-sweetened 70% dark chocolate, chopped

½ tablespoon coconut oil

½ tablespoon flaky sea salt

1. Mix together the peanut butter, butter, Swerve Confectioners, vanilla, stevia glycerite, and salt in a medium bowl.

2. Melt the chocolate and coconut oil together in a double boiler or microwave.

3. Line a muffin tray with 12 paper liners. Use a pastry brush to brush melted chocolate on the bottom and ¾ of the way up the sides of the paper liners (there should be melted chocolate left over). Freeze to solidify the chocolate, about 10 minutes.

4. Divide the peanut butter mixture between the 12 cups. Tap the tray on the countertop a few times to help spread out the peanut butter. Freeze to stiffen the peanut butter mixture, about 15 minutes.

5. Spoon the remaining chocolate on top of the peanut butter layers. Freeze 5 minutes to semi-set the chocolate, and then sprinkle the flaky sea salt on top.

6. Freeze or refrigerate to set the chocolate.

7. Store covered in the fridge for up to 1 month.

NOTE

Peanut Butter: the only ingredients should be peanuts and salt.

Cinnamon Roll Fat Bombs

YIELDS 12 FAT BOMBS | PREP TIME: 25 MINUTES | COOK TIME: N/A

Fat Bombs

½ cup raw unsalted sunflower
  seeds

¼ cup Swerve Confectioners

2⅛ teaspoons cinnamon,
  divided

⅛ teaspoon salt

4 ounces cream cheese

2 tablespoons unsalted butter

1 teaspoon pure vanilla extract

⅛ teaspoon stevia glycerite

1 cup almond flour

Icing

½ ounce cacao butter

1 ounce cream cheese, at room
  temperature

½ teaspoon pure vanilla extract

7 drops liquid stevia

½ tablespoon Swerve
  Confectioners

1. Add the sunflower seeds to a food processor and process until it forms fine crumbs, but don't let it form sunflower seed butter. Add the Swerve Confectioners, 2 teaspoons cinnamon, and salt and pulse a few times to combine.

2. Add the cream cheese, butter, vanilla, and stevia glycerite, and process until smooth.

3. Add the almond flour and process until smooth, stopping to scrape down the sides as necessary.

4. Spoon the mixture into a bowl and place a piece of plastic wrap directly on top. Refrigerate until fully chilled, about 4 hours.

5. Roll the dough into 12 equal balls (each just under 2 tablespoons). Chill in the freezer 10 minutes.

6. While the fat bomb balls are chilling in the freezer, make the icing. Melt the cacao butter in the microwave or a double boiler. Whisk in the cream cheese, and then all remaining ingredients.

7. Drizzle the icing on top of the fat bombs. Sprinkle on remaining ⅛ teaspoon cinnamon. Let the icing set before serving.

8. Store in an airtight container in the fridge for up to 2 weeks (these will soften quite a bit at room temperature).

DESSERTS

Blueberry Cheesecake Cups

Blueberry Sauce

1 cup fresh blueberries, plus 10 more for garnish (2 per serving) if desired

½ tablespoon erythritol

½ teaspoon pure vanilla extract

¼ teaspoon real fruit natural pectin

1 drop stevia glycerite

Vanilla Cheesecake Mousse

8 ounces (227 g) full-fat organic grass-fed cream cheese

2 tablespoons erythritol

1 teaspoon pure vanilla extract

3 drops stevia glycerite

1 cup (237 ml) organic grass-fed heavy whipping cream

1. Puree all ingredients for the blueberry sauce in a food processor (it doesn't have to be completely smooth), and set aside. The blueberry sauce will thicken slightly as it sits.

2. To make the vanilla cheesecake mousse, unwrap the cream cheese, place it in a large bowl, and microwave on high for 30 seconds to soften it. Add the erythritol, vanilla, and stevia glycerite and beat with a handheld electric mixer until smooth.

3. Beat the heavy cream to stiff peaks in a separate medium bowl. Beat ¼ of the whipped cream into the cream cheese mixture until smooth. Use a rubber spatula to fold in the remaining whipped cream ¼ at a time.

4. Transfer the mousse to 5 individual glasses or bowls and divide the blueberry sauce on top. Garnish each with 2 blueberries if desired.

5. Serve, or cover and keep refrigerated up to 3 days before serving.

Brownies

YIELDS 1 (8 BY 8-INCH) PAN, 12 SERVINGS | PREP TIME: 17 MINUTES
COOK TIME: 17 MINUTES

½ cup unsweetened runny almond butter

¼ cup avocado oil

¼ cup water

1 large egg

2 large egg yolks

1½ teaspoons pure vanilla extract

½ teaspoon espresso powder dissolved in 1 teaspoon boiling water

¼ teaspoon stevia glycerite

⅓ cup unsweetened natural cocoa powder

½ cup Swerve Confectioners

¼ teaspoon salt

¼ teaspoon baking powder

2 tablespoons stevia-sweetened chocolate chips

1. Preheat oven to 350°F; line an 8 by 8-inch baking pan with parchment paper.

2. Beat together the almond butter, oil, water, egg, egg yolks, vanilla, dissolved espresso, and stevia glycerite in a large bowl.

3. Sift in the cocoa powder, Swerve Confectioners, salt, and baking powder and mix to combine (the batter will be thick).

4. Spread the batter into the prepared baking pan and sprinkle the chocolate chips on top.

5. Bake for 15 to 17 minutes, 15 for gooey brownies and 17 for more set, but these taste better on the gooier side. If you let these brownies cook until a wooden pick comes out dry, they'll be overcooked.

6. Cool completely before cutting.

Chewy Chocolate Chip Cookies

YIELDS 8 COOKIES, 8 SERVINGS | PREP TIME: 25 MINUTES | COOK TIME: 15 MINUTES

1½ cups (168 g) almond flour

1 tablespoon beef gelatin (we used Vital Proteins)

1 teaspoon baking powder

¼ teaspoon fine salt

½ cup (113 g) grass-fed butter, melted and cooled slightly

⅓ cup (48 g) Swerve Confectioners

2 teaspoons pure vanilla extract

1 teaspoon blackstrap molasses

1 large egg

½ cup stevia-sweetened chocolate chips or chunks

1. Whisk together the almond flour, gelatin, baking powder, and salt in a medium bowl and set aside.

2. Beat together the melted butter and Swerve, and then beat in the vanilla and molasses, and finally the egg.

3. Stir the dry ingredients to the wet, and then fold in the chocolate chips.

4. Cover the bowl and refrigerate the dough 20 minutes. Meanwhile, preheat oven to 350°F; line 2 large baking sheets with parchment paper or Silpat liners.

5. Divide the dough into 8 portions and roll each into a ball. Arrange them on the baking sheets, slightly flattening each (leave quite a bit of space between each because the cookies spread out). Bake until the cookies are golden on the bottom and around the outside, about 15 minutes.

6. Cool completely on the trays before removing.

Brownie in a Mug

YIELDS 1 SERVING | PREP TIME: 3 MINUTES | COOK TIME: 2 MINUTES

2 tablespoons unsalted butter, melted in a microwave-safe mug and cooled slightly

2 tablespoons Lakanto maple-flavored syrup

1 tablespoon Lakanto granulated sugar substitute

7 drops liquid stevia

½ teaspoon pure vanilla extract

1 large egg

2 tablespoons almond flour

2 tablespoons unsweetened cocoa powder

1 tablespoon golden flaxseed meal

¼ teaspoon baking powder

1 pinch salt

1. In a regular-sized coffee mug, use a fork to combine together the butter, Lakanto syrup, granulated Lakanto, liquid stevia, vanilla, and egg. Add the almond flour, cocoa powder, flaxseed meal, baking powder, and salt and mix to combine.

2. Microwave on high for 1 minute 30 seconds.

3. Serve warm.

Devil's Food Cupcakes with Crème Fraîche Frosting

YIELDS 12 CUPCAKES | PREP TIME: 30 MINUTES | COOK TIME: 25 MINUTES

Devil's Food Cupcakes

6 tablespoons unsalted butter, at room temperature

⅔ cup Swerve Confectioners

2 large eggs

½ cup water

¼ cup heavy whipping cream

1½ teaspoons pure vanilla extract

½ teaspoon instant espresso powder dissolved in 1 teaspoon boiling water

¼ teaspoon stevia glycerite

1 cup almond flour

½ cup unsweetened natural cocoa powder (not Dutch-processed)

2 tablespoons coconut flour

½ teaspoon baking soda

½ teaspoon baking powder

¼ teaspoon salt

Crème Fraîche Frosting

4 tablespoons unsalted butter, at room temperature

¼ cup crème fraîche

½ ounce cacao butter, melted

1 pinch salt

½ teaspoon vanilla bean paste

¾ cup Swerve Confectioners

1. For the cupcakes, preheat the oven to 325°F and line a muffin tray with 12 paper liners.

2. Cream together the butter and Swerve Confectioners in a large bowl, and then cream in the eggs, water, heavy whipping cream, vanilla, dissolved espresso powder, and stevia glycerite.

3. Whisk together the almond flour, cocoa powder, coconut flour, baking soda, baking powder, and salt in a medium bowl.

4. Stir the dry ingredients into the wet and let the batter rest for 2 minutes.

5. Divide the batter into the lined muffin wells. Bake until a wooden pick inserted in the center of a cupcake comes out clean or with just a couple crumbs, about 25 minutes. Cool completely before frosting.

6. For the frosting, mix the butter and crème fraîche into the melted, still warm cacao butter. Stir in the salt and vanilla bean paste, and then the Swerve Confectioners. Cool to room temperature, and then place a piece of plastic wrap directly on top of the frosting and chill 30 minutes in the fridge (the frosting will stiffen a bit).

7. Beat the frosting with a handheld electric mixer until smooth, and then frost the cupcakes.

8. The frosting will soften at room temperature and stiffen in the fridge, so store the cupcakes in an airtight container in the fridge for up to 1 week. Let them sit at room temperature for about 10 minutes before serving.

Chocolate Cheesecake Mousse

YIELDS 6 SERVINGS | PREP TIME: 10 MINUTES | COOK TIME: N/A

8 ounces (227 g) full-fat organic cream cheese

1 teaspoon granulated stevia or your sweetener of choice, more or less to taste

1 teaspoon pure vanilla extract

½ teaspoon vanilla bean paste (or an additional ½ teaspoon pure vanilla extract)

1 cup (237 ml) heavy cream

1½ ounces stevia-sweetened dark chocolate, grated or very finely chopped

1. Unwrap the cream cheese, place it in a large bowl, and microwave on high for 30 seconds to soften it. Add the stevia, vanilla extract, and vanilla bean paste and beat with a handheld electric mixer until smooth.

2. Beat the heavy cream to stiff peaks in a medium bowl. Beat ¼ of the whipped cream into the cream cheese mixture until smooth. Use a rubber spatula to fold in the remaining whipped cream ¼ at a time, and then fold in the grated chocolate.

3. Transfer the mousse to 6 individual glasses or bowls.

4. Serve, or cover and keep refrigerated up to 3 days before serving.

Raspberry Gelatin
with Fresh Whipped Cream

YIELDS 5 SERVINGS | PREP TIME: 10 MINUTES | COOK TIME: N/A

6 ounces unsweetened frozen red raspberries, thawed

2 tablespoons unflavored beef gelatin

2 cups boiling water

2 tablespoons granulated erythritol

1 teaspoon fresh lemon juice

½ teaspoon stevia glycerite

1 pinch salt

½ cup heavy whipping cream, whipped to soft peaks

1. Puree the raspberries in a blender and pour into a large bowl.

2. Stir the gelatin into the raspberries and let it stand for 1 minute.

3. Whisk in the boiling water and erythritol until the gelatin and erythritol are dissolved.

4. Stir in the lemon juice, stevia glycerite, and salt.

5. Pour into small cups and refrigerate until set.

6. Serve each with a dollop of fresh whipped cream on top.

Pictured: Coconut Hazelnut Espresso Chocolate Bark

Coconut Hazelnut Espresso Chocolate Bark

YIELDS 6 SERVINGS | PREP TIME: 10 MINUTES | COOK TIME: N/A

2 (3-oz/85-g) stevia-sweetened dark chocolate bars

2 tablespoons unsalted roasted hazelnuts, chopped

2 tablespoons unsweetened coconut flakes

½ tablespoon cacao nibs

½ teaspoon coarse coffee grinds

1. Line a large baking sheet with parchment paper.

2. Melt the chocolate in a double boiler or microwave.

3. Spread the chocolate out on the prepared baking sheet until it's about ¼-inch thick.

4. Sprinkle on the hazelnuts, coconut flakes, cacao nibs, and coffee.

5. Let the chocolate set and then break it into pieces. Store it in an airtight container in the fridge for up to 1 month.

Chocolate Avocado Ice Cream Pops

YIELDS 12 | PREP TIME: 10 MINUTES | COOK TIME: N/A

3 small Haas avocados, seed and skin removed

1 (13½-oz) can organic unsweetened full-fat coconut milk

½ cup unsweetened cocoa powder

½ cup Swerve Confectioners

1½ teaspoons pure vanilla extract

½ teaspoon stevia glycerite

½ teaspoon espresso extract

½ teaspoon fresh lemon juice

1 pinch salt

1. Add all ingredients to a blender or food processor and process until smooth.

2. Pour the mixture into 12 (75-ml/2½-oz) ice pop molds, making sure not to fill the molds over the "fill" line. Tap the mold several times on a hard surface to help any air bubbles escape.

3. Transfer to the freezer, wait 20 minutes, and then insert the sticks. Let the pops freeze completely, about 3 to 4 hours.

4. To easily unmold the pops, dip the plastic bottoms in warm water and they should slide right out.

5. Wrap each pop individually in plastic wrap and store in the freezer for up to 3 months.

Almond Butter Chocolate Chunk Cookies

YIELDS 11 COOKIES, 11 SERVINGS | PREP TIME: 18 MINUTES | COOK TIME: 12 MINUTES

1 cup (256 g) creamy unsweetened almond butter

1 large egg

1 teaspoon pure vanilla extract

¼ teaspoon salt

⅓ cup (48 g) Swerve Confectioners

1.2 ounces (35 g) stevia-sweetened dark chocolate, cut into 11 squares

1. Preheat oven to 350°F; line a large baking sheet with parchment paper or a Silpat liner.

2. Add the almond butter to the bowl of a food processor and process until no lumps remain.

3. Add the egg, vanilla, and salt, and process to combine, scraping down the sides as necessary.

4. Add the Swerve and process until it comes together as a ball of dough.

5. Measure out 2-tablespoon-sized scoops of dough, roll each into a ball, and arrange the dough balls evenly on the baking sheet.

6. Lightly press a piece of chocolate into the center of each ball of dough.

7. Bake until the cookies are golden on the bottom and outside, about 12 minutes.

8. Cool the cookies on the tray before removing and serving.

DRINKS

Fatty Matcha

YIELDS 1 SERVING | PREP TIME: 10 MINUTES | COOK TIME: N/A

1 cup + 2 tablespoons (9 oz) boiling water

1½ teaspoons good-quality organic matcha powder

1 tablespoon organic coconut oil

1 tablespoon organic ghee

1 teaspoon pure vanilla extract

1 small pinch sea salt

1 (1-g) packet stevia/erythritol blend

1. Add all ingredients to a blender and process until smooth and creamy.

2. Serve immediately.

Fatty Earl Grey Tea

YIELDS 1 SERVING | PREP TIME: 5 MINUTES | COOK TIME: N/A

1 cup strong hot brewed Earl Grey tea

1 tablespoon grass-fed butter

1 tablespoon MCT oil

3 drops culinary-grade orange essential oil (optional)

3 drops liquid stevia

1. Add all ingredients to a blender and process until smooth and creamy.

2. Serve.

Fatty Bone Broth

YIELDS 1 SERVING | PREP TIME: 5 MINUTES | COOK TIME: N/A

1 cup homemade or top-quality store-bought chicken bone broth, warmed to simmering

2 tablespoons salted grass-fed butter

1. Blend the broth and butter in a blender until foamy.

2. Serve immediately.

Strawberry Milkshake

YIELDS 1 SERVING | PREP TIME: 5 MINUTES | COOK TIME: N/A

¼ cup heavy whipping cream

½ cup water

1 (1-g) packet stevia/erythritol blend

1 teaspoon pure vanilla extract

1 pinch salt

½ cup frozen sliced strawberries

½ cup ice cubes

1. Add the cream, water, stevia/erythritol blend, vanilla, and salt to a blender and pulse to combine.

2. Add the frozen strawberries and ice cubes and process until smooth and creamy, tamping down as necessary. Don't overmix or the milkshake will be watery.

3. Pour into a serving glass and serve immediately.

Fatty Cinnamon-Spiced Coffee

YIELDS 1 SERVING | PREP TIME: 5 MINUTES | COOK TIME: N/A

8 ounces hot, brewed coffee

1 tablespoon unrefined coconut oil

1 tablespoon unsalted grass-fed butter

1 pinch cinnamon

1. Blend all ingredients until smooth and frothy.

2. Serve.

Chocolate Mint Milkshake

YIELDS 1 SERVING | PREP TIME: 5 MINUTES | COOK TIME: N/A

1 tablespoon chia seeds

¼ cup heavy whipping cream

½ cup water

2 tablespoons natural unsweetened cocoa powder

¾ teaspoon pure vanilla extract

¼ teaspoon pure peppermint extract

1 pinch sea salt

2 (1-g) packets granulated stevia/erythritol blend

1 cup ice cubes

2 tablespoons heavy whipping cream whipped to soft peaks, for garnish

1 fresh mint leaf, for garnish

1. Add the chia seeds to a high-speed blender and process until it turns powdery.

2. To the blender, add the cream, water, cocoa powder, vanilla, peppermint extract, salt, and granulated stevia/erythritol and pulse to combine.

3. Add the ice cubes and pulse until smooth (be careful not to overmix so your smoothie stays thick).

4. Transfer to a serving glass. Top with the whipped cream and a mint leaf and serve immediately.

Lemon Coconut Smoothie

YIELDS 1 SERVING | PREP TIME: 5 MINUTES | COOK TIME: N/A

1 tablespoon white chia seeds

½ cup plain unsweetened almond milk

¼ cup canned unsweetened full-fat coconut milk

1 teaspoon fresh lemon zest

¾ teaspoon pure vanilla extract

½ teaspoon fresh lemon juice

1 pinch sea salt

1 (1-g) packet granulated stevia/erythritol blend

1½ cups ice cubes

2½ tablespoons unsweetened coconut flakes, divided

2 tablespoons heavy whipping cream whipped to soft peaks, for garnish

1. Add the chia seeds to a high-speed blender and process until it turns powdery.

2. To the blender, add the almond milk, coconut milk, lemon zest, vanilla, lemon juice, salt, and granulated stevia/erythritol and process until smooth.

3. Add the ice cubes and pulse until smooth (be careful not to overmix so your smoothie stays thick). Stir in 2 tablespoons coconut flakes.

4. Transfer to a serving glass. Top with the whipped cream and remaining ½ tablespoon coconut flakes and serve immediately.

ABOUT THE AUTHORS

Faith is a lawyer turned food stylist, photographer, and recipe developer specializing in low-carb and ketogenic recipes. She owns the food blogs An Edible Mosaic and Healthy Sweet Eats. After spending an extensive amount of time traveling, she is also a published author of a traditional Middle Eastern cookbook, *An Edible Mosaic: Middle Eastern Fare with Extraordinary Flair*. Lara is a registered dietitian nutritionist, personal trainer, and keto coach. Faith and Lara are the founders of the website The Keto Queens: www.theketoqueens.com.

CONVERSION CHARTS

Metric and Imperial Conversions

(These conversions are rounded for convenience)

Ingredient	Cups/Tablespoons/Teaspoons	Ounces	Grams/Milliliters
Butter	1 cup/ 16 tablespoons/ 2 sticks	8 ounces	230 grams
Cheese, shredded	1 cup	4 ounces	110 grams
Cream cheese	1 tablespoon	0.5 ounce	14.5 grams
Fruit, dried	1 cup	4 ounces	120 grams
Fruits or veggies, chopped	1 cup	5 to 7 ounces	145 to 200 grams
Fruits or veggies, pureed	1 cup	8.5 ounces	245 grams
Liquids: cream, milk, water, or juice	1 cup	8 fluid ounces	240 milliliters
Salt	1 teaspoon	0.2 ounce	6 grams
Spices: cinnamon, cloves, ginger, or nutmeg (ground)	1 teaspoon	0.2 ounce	5 milliliters
Vanilla extract	1 teaspoon	0.2 ounce	4 grams

Oven Temperatures

Fahrenheit	Celsius	Gas Mark
225°	110°	¼
250°	120°	½
275°	140°	1
300°	150°	2
325°	160°	3
350°	180°	4
375°	190°	5
400°	200°	6
425°	220°	7
450°	230°	8

RECIPE LIST

INDEX

Notes

Notes

Notes

Notes